S0-AIO-546

STUDIO SECRETS

646.5
R

C-1

STUDIO SECRETS
MILLINERY

Estelle Ramousse
Fabienne Gambrelle

Photography
Florent de La Tullaye

DISCARD
STAUNTON PUBLIC LIBRARY

SEARCH PRESS

FOREWORD

Estelle Ramousse's career was triggered by a trip to the circus with her grandmother at the age of four. Filled with wonder at the sight of the circus performers, she decided that one day she would work in the realm of stage productions. The idea started to take shape when she became a teenager and was invited to a fancy dress ball. Estelle spent an entire night at her sewing machine making a headdress. The next day, she told her parents that she knew what she wanted to do in life: make hats! The young milliner learned her trade part-time at Rue de Courcelles, Paris, in the workshop of Christiane and Marinette Bernardini. As soon as she achieved her certificate in vocational training (CAP) at the Chambre Syndicale de la Couture Parisienne in 1989, she began to devote herself to her two passions: stage production and fashion. In 1992, she designed the black headdresses for the singers in 'Rodrigue et Chimène', produced by Georges Lavaudant at the Opera House in Lyons. In 1995, she was one of the milliners who worked with Alfredo Arias when he staged 'Fou des Folies' at the Folies-Bergère. From 1999 to 2002, Estelle went on a world tour with the show 'Triptyk' by the equestrian theatre Zingaro. At the same time, she was making hats for the prêt-à-porter (Gilles Rosier, 1998) and haute couture (Stéphanie Coudert, 2004) stylists.

Estelle is now a prosperous and highly respected milliner. She lives in the 20th arrondissement of Paris, where she designs bespoke hats and continues to give expression to her dual passions: the stage and fashion. The roots of her talent lie in the fact that she has a great feel for fabric, but perhaps it would be better to quote the words of the great milliner Claude Saint-Cyr, who said that milliners 'can make anything with their hands'; according to this definition, Estelle Ramousse is a milliner *par excellence*.

08

HISTORY OF
THE TRADE

16

WORKSHOP VISIT

THE WORKSHOP
THE TOOLS
THE MATERIALS

AT MADAME GALANTER'S

28

EXPERTISE

THE BASIC TECHNIQUES

- CUT AND SEWN
- CUSTOMISATION
- MAKING HAT FRAMES

110

THE CREATIVE ARTIST

- CROWN OF FLOWERS
- CHINESE-STYLE CAP
- BERET
- BIBI
- WIDE-BRIMMED HAT
- WOOLLY HAT
- FEDORA
- CLOCHE

A MILLINER'S SHOP FRONT (1914), AUGUST MACKE, LEOPOLD HOESCH MUSEUM, DÜREN, GERMANY

HISTORY
OF THE TRADE

In the past, milliners' shop signs were commonplace in French towns. In the 18th century, the centre of elegance was the Palais-Royal, one of the most beautiful gardens in Paris, surrounded by arcades of shops. In the 19th century, the centre of fashion moved over towards the Grands Boulevards and the Opéra. In the following century, it moved on to Rue Saint-Honoré and the Champs-Elysées circus.

Nowadays, it is rare to see a milliner's shop front in a French town. Since the mid fifties, the wearing of hats has fallen out of fashion. Cars, sport, casual hairstyles and a desire for the practical mean that hats, which used to be *de rigueur*, have now become redundant. Luckily, the great couturiers and some talented milliners working in fashion, stage productions or for private clients, are perpetuating the great tradition of the hat, which had its heyday from 1850 to 1950.

The hat, or headdress, dates back to the beginning of the history of mankind. Human beings have always covered their heads to protect them from inclement weather and from the sun. In more recent times, headwear has signified rank in society, an individual's power or a trade. In France, the *Coporation des Chapeliers* was formed in the Middle Ages. They made and sold hats for men, the shapes of which were sometimes borrowed by women, in addition to the gauze, lawn or lace bonnets that were made by the linen maids. Florists also made headpieces from fresh flowers worn as crowns at rural festivals.

The 18th century saw the arrival of the milliner who, according to the chronicler Louis-Sébastien Mercier, was to become the scourge of men. 'All husbands are afraid of fashion merchants and can only think of them with fear,' he wrote in 1783. 'As soon as the bachelor sees these hats, fitted clothes and styles that women idolise, he stops and thinks and then decides to remain a boy. Yet young women will say that they love commemorative pouf hats and bonnets as much as their husbands.'

In 1776, the fashion merchants, or milliners, teamed up with the florists, who made artificial flowers, and with the *plumassiers* who prepared the feathers. The milliners supplied all the fashion accessories, including the hats. Later, the making of hats was divided into two professions: the hatters, who made a series of limited-edition hats in designs for men, and the milliners, who invented 'enjoyable fashion' for women, in particular original hats that were often unique.

The first milliner to rise to fame was Rose Bertin, 'Minister of Fashion for Marie-Antoinette'. Some of her creations were so tall that they had to be equipped with springs to allow this fashionable woman to sit in her carriage! The height of hats was nothing new. In the Middle Ages, noble women wearing hennin bonnets were obliged to curtsey (against their will) when going through a door. Rose Bertin brought height back into fashion and added extravagance to it. She became famous for her pouf hats, which were a type of commemorative bonnet covered with decorations relevant to the time. For example, the 'inoculation' pouf was designed to commemorate the vaccination of King Louis XVI against smallpox, and the 'hot air' pouf to commemorate the flight of the Montgolfier brothers in their balloon, invented in 1783.

AT THE MILLINER'S (1898), EDGAR DEGAS, MUSÉE D'ORSAY, PARIS, FRANCE

Milliners prospered in the 19th century. They ruled over the fashion trade, gradually concentrating on making hats and giving up other fashion accessories. One of the most fashionable milliners was Caroline Reboux, working in the Rue de la Paix and then Avenue Matignon in Paris, who worked for the couturier Worth. Another, Marie Séguin, invented the pliable hat, equipped with springs, so that several hats could be arranged in the same box – the hat box that was typically used by milliners crossing town to deliver their work to their clients.

All that is left now of most of the local milliners are some faded hats, forgotten at the back of a wardrobe or in an attic. Others have been remembered because they became famous in another field, such as the café and concert hall singers Theresa and Yvette Guilbert, or because they opened their own fashion house, such as Jeanne Lanvin, Gabrielle Chanel or Elsa Schiaparelli. Like their colleagues, these milliners who became *grands couturiers* began learning their trade in the workshops that teamed with dozens of workers at the start of the 20th century. Initially, they were apprentices, i.e. appointed to the service of other milliners. During the first year of training, apprentices took on the role of runners: they remained on their feet, at the disposal of the more experienced milliners, who were sat around the table. Often, the work area was so covered with tools and materials that the milliners worked on the hats on their knees. First of all, the *apprêteuses* prepared the shape of the hat, then the *garnisseuses* added the decorative touches. The former played the most important role in the workshop. They proposed shapes to the proprietress, who remained the milliner and gave the hats her label. Such milliners included Esther Meyer, the Loys sisters, Marie-Alphonsine, Maria Guy, Jeanne Blanchot, the Legroux sisters, Rose Valois,

A YOUNG MILLINER IN THE STREETS OF PARIS (1892). JEAN BERAUD, BIBLIOTHÈQUE DES ARTS DÉCORATIFS, PARIS, FRANCE

Lucienne Rebaté, Gaby Mono, Blanche and Simone, Agnès, Georgette Lewis (who gave her name to a type of crêpe), Jeannette Colombier, known for her flower headdresses, Madeleine Panizon, milliner for Paul Poiret, Rose Descat who, in 1932, put Marlene Dietrich in a man's hat, and also Madame Suzy, whose *chapeaux de singe* and *petits choux* outraged the public in 1936.

In this great era of the hat, a number of suppliers worked exclusively for the sector: felt manufacturers, fabric and straw preparers, florists and *plumassiers* (who prepared ornamental feathers), haberdashers, blockmakers (who made the wooden blocks over which the felt hats were stretched), etc. Nowadays, the number of suppliers has fallen, like the number of milliners. Although Rose Valois remained active until the beginning of the seventies and Paulette, who in 1939 could be found in the Avenue Franklin-Roosevelt, worked for the cinema and haute couture until her death in 1984, the great workshops have disappeared, as has the division of tasks. Nowadays, milliners generally work alone in their workshops and have to be able to make any kind of hat. They work for some private clients, for stage productions and for fashion stylists. Fashion designers rarely expect their models to walk the cat-walk without a hat. And what other accessory perfects the silhouette better than a hat – by Stephen Jones or Philip Treacy, for example – veritable artists, whose inspirational work is particularly appreciated by Estelle Ramousse.

APPRENTICE MILLINERS IN 1946

WORKSHOP VISIT

IN 2004, ESTELLE RAMOUSSE SET UP HER WORKSHOP ON A STEEP LITTLE STREET IN THE HILLS OF BELLEVILLE. IN THE WINDOW, SHE PRESENTS HER SUMMER OR WINTER COLLECTIONS ACCORDING TO THE SEASONS. INSIDE, SHE WELCOMES HER CLIENTS AND MAKES HATS UNDER THE BENEVOLENT PROTECTION OF HINDU IDOLS, PLASTIC ELEPHANTS, POLYCHROME MASKS AND FLAMENCO DANCERS PINNED TO THE WALL.

THE WORKSHOP

IN ESTELLE'S WORKSHOP, JUST AS IN THE PALACE OF THE GREAT FILM DIRECTOR JEAN COCTEAU, HANDS COME OUT OF THE WALLS. HERE, THOUGH, THEY ARE MADE OF PLASTIC AND, RATHER THAN CARRYING TORCHES, THEY CARRY HATS. FOR THE FITTING, YOU MAY SIT IN A RATTAN CHAIR, IN FRONT OF A LARGE MIRROR LEANT AGAINST THE STONE WALL OF THE BOUTIQUE, WHICH RESEMBLES BOTH A FASHION HOUSE AND A DOLL'S HOUSE.

ESTELLE MOVES AWAY FROM HER SEWING MACHINE TO SHOW THE HAT SEEN IN THE WINDOW OR TO TAKE AN ORDER FOR THE BESPOKE HEADPIECE THAT HER CLIENT IS DREAMING OF. SHE ENTERS INTO HER VISITOR'S DREAM SO THAT SHE CAN MAKE IT COME TRUE. IN FRONT OF THE MIRROR, SHE IMPROVISES A HAT BLOCK WITH A PIANO STRING, GRABS A FEATHER, MATCHES THE MATERIALS, SPLITS THEM UP AND MARRIES THEM TOGETHER IN A DIFFERENT WAY.

SHE SHOWS A PILE OF FABRICS TO HER CLIENT, THROWING A SHINY STRAP OR SOME SHELLS OVER THE MOST SUITABLE PIECE. MULLING OVER HER IDEAS, ESTELLE LIGHTS A CIGARETTE. SUDDENLY, SHE KNOWS WHAT TO DO AND RUMMAGES THROUGH ONE OF THE METAL BOXES ARRANGED UNDER THE WINDOW. FROM AMONG ITS TREASURES, SHE COLLECTS THE INGREDIENTS FOR THE POTION. THERE'S SOMETHING OF A MAGIC FAIRY ABOUT A MILLINER, AND SOMETHING OF A SORCERER TOO (A VERY ROCK AND ROLL SORCERER IN ESTELLE'S CASE). THE HAT IS PUT TOGETHER LIKE A MAGIC SPELL; A SECRET POTION FOR STYLISH AND CHIC CREATIONS. AND ESTELLE EXCELS AT THIS: INFUSING HER EXPERTISE AND TALENT WITH A SENSE OF MAGIC.

THE TOOLS

IN ADDITION TO THE TAILORS' AND COUTURIERS' TOOLS AND MATERIALS FOUND IN THE WORKSHOP, THERE ARE ITEMS SPECIFIC TO MILLINERY. THE MODEL, OR DOLLY, FOR EXAMPLE, MADE FROM PAPIER-MÂCHÉ COVERED WITH TAILOR'S CLOTH, AND INTO WHICH PINS CAN BE INSERTED EASILY AT ALL STAGES IN THE CREATION OF A HAT.

YOU WILL ALSO FIND WOODEN HAT BLOCKS AND SPARTERIES FOR MOULDING FELT, STRAW OR FABRIC HATS. THE SPARTERIE IS A WOODEN FRAMEWORK COVERED IN STARCHED MUSLIN, CALLED *SINGALETTE*, MADE BY THE MILLINER FOR STRETCHING SOME TYPES OF HATS. THE SPARTERIE ACTS AS A BASE FOR THE BLOCKMAKER, OR *BOISIER*, TO MAKE THE MOULD WITH LIME TREE WOOD, WHICH IS PERMEABLE AND FLEXIBLE, AND INTO WHICH IT IS POSSIBLE TO STICK PINS.

ABOVE: SOME NEEDLES AND PINS ARE DESIGNED ESPECIALLY FOR MILLINERS. NO. 7 NEEDLES IN THE SPECIAL 'MILLINER' SERIES BY BOHIN ARE LONGER THAN NORMAL NEEDLES, MAKING IT EASIER TO SEW INSIDE A HAT. OTHER PINS ARE ALSO DESIGNED FOR MILLINERY. CAMIONS ARE MINISCULE PINS THAT MILLINERS USE TO SECURE THE ROLLS OF GROSGRAIN RIBBON. T-PINS, PLACED HERE NEXT TO A CHALK HEM MARKER, WHICH IS USED FOR DRAWING ON FABRICS. T-PINS ARE LARGE PINS DESIGNED FOR USE WHEN STRETCHING FELT AND CLOTH OVER WOOD. THESE PINS ARE LONG AND FLEXIBLE AND THEY CAN BE BENT USING A HAMMER ONCE THEY ARE IN PLACE.

ABOVE, RIGHT: IN ADDITION TO A HAMMER, MILLINERS SOMETIMES ALSO NEED A WEIGHT. THEY ALSO USE IRONS INCLUDING: NORMAL IRONS; IRONS FROM POLAND, WHICH ARE LITTLE IRONS THAT ENABLE ACCESS TO NARROW OR ROUNDED PARTS OF THE HAT; AND *COQ* IRONS OR *COQS* (SHOWN BETWEEN THE HAMMER AND THE WEIGHT), WITH AN OVAL END FOR STRETCHING THE HOT FELT OR CLOTH OVER A BLOCK OR SPARTERIE. THE CIRCULAR TOOL (RIGHT) IS FOR MEASURING THE HEAD OPENING OF A HAT, I.E. THE SIZE OF THE HAT.

RIGHT: ANOTHER SPECIALIST TOOL USED BY MILLINERS IS THE HAT STRETCHER, WHICH ENABLES THE SIZE OF THE HAT TO BE INCREASED. SOME OTHER WELL-KNOWN TOOLS ARE USED WHEN PRESENTING OR ARRANGING HATS: HAT STANDS, FOR WHICH ESTELLE SOMETIMES IMPROVISES BY USING ENGRAVED GLASS MODELS OF THE EIFFEL TOWER, AND HAT BOXES, WHICH ARE BECOMING INCREASINGLY RARE AS THEY ARE EXTREMELY EXPENSIVE.

THE MATERIALS

MATERIALS ARE SCATTERED THROUGHOUT THE WORKSHOP: BOBBINS OF THREAD ARE LINED UP ON THE SEWING MACHINE TABLE, NEXT TO A MINIATURE CHAIR (LEFT PHOTO); FABRICS ARE PILED UP ON A WOODEN TRESTLE; STRAW HATS ARE PILED ON A SEAT AFTER A PRESENTATION TO A CLIENT (RIGHT PHOTO); RIBBONS AND LACE ARE STUFFED INTO BOXES AND SLIPPED BENEATH THE WINDOW, WITH PIECES OF LEATHER, FLOWERS AND ARTIFICIAL FRUITS, OR EVEN FEATHERS.

ABOVE, LEFT: ESTELLE PREFERS TO USE PEACOCK AND COCKEREL FEATHERS, AS WELL AS NANDOU FEATHERS FROM THE LARGE SOUTH AMERICAN BIRD SIMILAR TO AN OSTRICH, AND THOSE OF THE EGRET, A WHITE HERON WITH TAPERING FEATHERS. THE WORD 'EGRET' ALSO MEANS A PLUME OF FEATHERS ON TOP OF THE HEAD OF SOME FOWL, AS WELL AS A DECORATIVE PLUME ATTACHED TO A HAT.

ABOVE, RIGHT: NUMEROUS TYPES OF SILK FLOWERS ARE AVAILABLE FROM ARTNUPTIA, AND OTHER SPECIALIST MILLINERY SUPPLIERS. THEY ARE MADE USING MOULDS THAT ENABLE ANY TYPE OF PETAL OR LEAF TO BE REPRODUCED, DEPENDING ON THE DESIRED FLOWER. IN THE PAST, WORKERS OFTEN MADE THEM IN THEIR OWN HOMES AND SPECIALISED IN ONE TYPE OF FLOWER. ROSE BUSHES WERE THE PINNACLE OF THIS CRAFTSMANSHIP, WITH THE ROSE BEING ONE OF THE MOST DIFFICULT FLOWERS TO IMITATE. SOME CRAFTSMEN ONLY MADE THE FOLIAGE: THEY WERE CALLED *FEUILLAGISTES* OR *VERDURIERS*.

LEFT: THE ART OF THE *PLUMASSIER*, WHO PREPARES AND DYES THE FEATHERS, IS SOMETIMES LIKENED TO THAT OF A TAXIDERMIST, AS SHOWN BY THE PHOTO OF THIS PHEASANT, SOLD BY ARTNUPTIA – FORMERLY CHAVET, HOUSE OF FABRICS AND FASHION – WHERE ESTELLE BUYS SOME OF HER SUPPLIES. THERE SHE FINDS THREADS, STIFFENING FABRICS (STARCHED MUSLIN, FLANNELETTE AND ADHESIVE WEBBING), CRINS, MILLINERY WIRE, FELT, STRAW HATS, VARIOUS FABRICS, GROSGRAIN RIBBONS AND OTHER TRIMMINGS, LACE, VIOLETS, FLOWERS, FRUITS, FEATHERS, ETC. REQUIRED FOR MAKING HATS AND THEIR DECORATIONS.

AT MADAME GALANTER'S

WHEN ESTELLE NEEDS SOME ADVICE, OR PERHAPS A BLOCK FOR STRETCHING A HAT, SHE GOES TO MADAME ALBERTINE GALANTER, WHO IS 92 YEARS OLD AND FOR WHOM SHE HAS GREAT RESPECT AND AFFECTION. MADAME GALANTER WILLINGLY HELPS ESTELLE AND PROVIDES HER WITH MATERIALS. IN PARTICULAR, SHE ALLOWS HER TO SEARCH THROUGH HER COLLECTION OF BLOCKS (SHOWN OPPOSITE) THAT REFLECT HALF A CENTURY OF HAT FASHIONS. MADAME GALANTER OPENED A BOUTIQUE ON THE RUE DES FRANCS-BOURGEOIS IN THE 4TH ARRONDISSEMENT OF PARIS IMMEDIATELY AFTER THE SECOND WORLD WAR. FROM THAT FIRST WORKSHOP, WITH SOME HELPERS, SHE WORKED BOTH FOR PRIVATE CLIENTS AND FOR OTHER MILLINERS, INCLUDING DANIEL MASSON. THE DECLINE IN THE TRADE IN THE FIFTIES MEANT THAT SHE HAD TO CLOSE THE BOUTIQUE AND WORK FROM HOME AT NO. 9 BOULEVARD RICHARD-LENOIR. MADAME GALANTER CONTINUES TO MAKE HATS FOR A SELECT CLIENTELE, INCLUDING THE FAMOUS MADAME DE FONTENAY.

MADAME ALBERTINE GALANTER IN FRONT OF A LAMBSKIN CLOCHE MADE BY HER, PRESENTED ON A WOODEN DOLLY – A RARITY, AS DOLLY HEADS WERE GENERALLY MADE OF PAPIER-MÂCHÉ. THIS WAS A PRESENT FROM MADAME GALANTER'S BLOCKMAKER, TINO RE.

OPPOSITE: THE SHELVES ARE LINED WITH SPARTERIES AND DOLLY HEADS – SOME OF THEM WEARING A MANCHON, A TYPE OF BONNET INTENDED TO ENLARGE THE SIZE OF THE HEAD.

MADAME GALANTER'S SEWING MACHINE BELONGED TO HER WET NURSE WHO, DURING THE FIRST WORLD WAR, USED IT TO MAKE CAPS FOR THE FRENCH SOLDIERS. MADAME GALANTER GOT INTO THE HABIT OF SEWING STANDING UP. SHE IRONED SITTING DOWN, AS WAS DONE IN THE PAST IN THE MILLINERS' WORKSHOPS, WITH A BOARD RESTING ON HER KNEES AND HER FEET RESTING ON A LITTLE FOOTSTOOL.

EXPERTISE

FOR ESTELLE, A SINGLE 'HEAD FOR HATS' DOES NOT
EXIST, EVEN IF ALL THE HATS SHE CREATES FIT LIKE A
GLOVE! YOU NEED TO WORK OUT THE SHAPE OF HAT
THAT WILL SUIT YOUR FACE AND YOUR STYLE. TRY
THEM OUT, LOOK AROUND AND DARE TO WEAR! HERE
ARE SOME IDEAS FOR MAKING THE KINDS OF HATS
YOU WOULD LIKE TO HAVE, OR FOR CUSTOMISING
THOSE THAT YOU ALREADY OWN.

1

THE BASIC TECHNIQUES

CUT AND SEWN

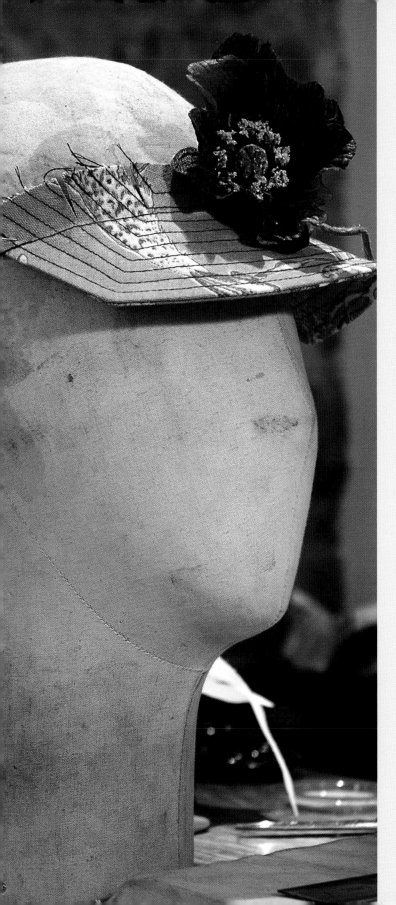

The cut-and-sewn technique enables hats to be made simply by sewing. Estelle learned to sew during her apprenticeship, but during her childhood she also attended sewing classes given to her mother by her great aunt. Whilst the two women were at the sewing machine, Estelle used to play with scraps of fabric, bits of ribbon and buttons that she would put together in unusual combinations. The memories of these afternoons and the smell of afternoon tea taken whilst talking of fabrics and patterns, as the light faded outside and sometimes as the rain began to fall, came back to her with every stitch sewn in her workshop in the Rue de la Mare.

Crown of flowers

This circlet, or headband, is made using a combination of découpage, collage and the cut-and-sewn technique. Instead of buying fabric or paper flowers, or even re-using the decorations from an old hat, Estelle suggests making the flowers in cotton fabric printed with a floral motif.

PATTERN FOR A FLOWER

1. Cut out four flowers (two large and two small) from the printed fabric, then cut around the flowers, leaving a small margin around the petals.

→ *Use sharp dressmaking scissors.*

2. Take some adhesive webbing (available in two colours: black and white) in the colour that goes best with your fabric. Place the flowers on to the adhesive side. The webbing is only adhesive on one side: the lightest side (you can also tell by touching it). Iron (without steam): the dry heat will make the flower stick to the adhesive webbing, which will stiffen it and prevent the fabric from fraying. Protect the cotton by covering it with another piece of cloth and ironing over that. Use a very hot iron, and iron until the flower is stuck firmly to the webbing. If the flowers are cut from synthetic fabric, set the iron to a medium heat (following the recommendations given on the thermostat of your iron).

→ *Do not use steam or a damp cloth to fix the fabric to the adhesive webbing.*

3. Carefully cut out the flowers following the contours of the motif. Iron over them again, on the reverse this time. This will enable you to re-stick any adhesive webbing that may have come away from the fabric when you were cutting out the flowers. It will also prevent the fabric from fraying.

4. Pin the flowers on to the dolly (or model) and decide on the position and final number of flowers for the decoration.

MAKING THE HEADBAND

1. Move on to making the headband itself, on to which the flowers will be attached. Measure over your head from one ear to the other with a tape measure. Estelle makes her headband from elastic and it is worn over loose hair.

→ *If you prefer to wear the headband over a ponytail or a chignon, make a headband without elastic, measuring the same as the complete circumference of your head.*

2. Cut out a headband from pattern card to fit over your head. Decide on the width of the headband; here, it is 7cm (2¾in). Leave a margin of 1cm (½in) at each end. Mark this 1cm (½in) seam allowance with a pencil on each end of the headband, and draw a line across the centre of the headband.

3. Hang the card over a model, making the line across the middle of the headband line up with the mark on the dolly that indicates the centre of the forehead. Check that the proportions are right. If the flowers are large, you will need a wider headband. If the flowers are small, you can cut out a narrower headband. Once you are happy with the headband, make some notches in the pattern card in the seam allowances and in the middle of the headband (make notches by cutting out little triangles in the card, with two snips of the scissors, using the points of the blades).

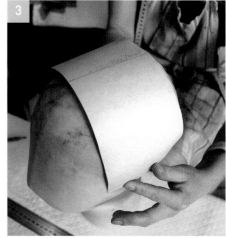

4. There are two directions to any fabric: the straight grain and the bias. In millinery, the fabric is always worked on the bias, so that it will mould to fit the shape of the head.

To find the bias, fold the selvage of the fabric (i.e. the finished edge) over at a 90-degree angle. Pull on the fabric using your thumb and forefinger: if it stretches, you are on the full bias. On the straight grain, the fabric does not move – it has no elasticity.

5. Cut the fabric to the measurements of the card, leaving a small margin, and placing a weight on the pattern to prevent the fabric from moving underneath.

Cut a piece of adhesive webbing to the measurements of the fabric, leaving a small margin, as for the flower. Cut the adhesive webbing on the bias, i.e. in the direction of stretch of the fabric.

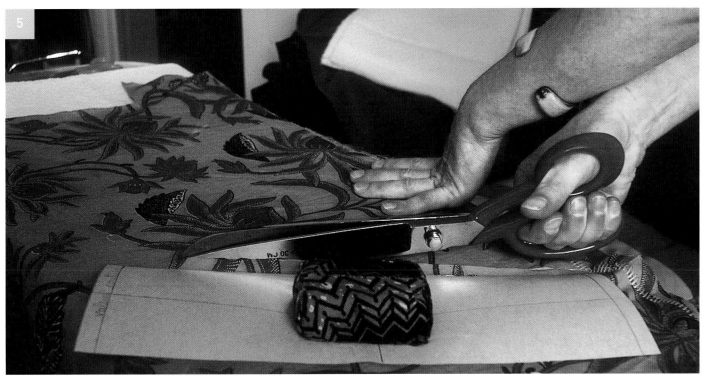

1. Attach the fabric to the adhesive webbing by ironing over it; check that it is spread flat on to the webbing and that there are no creases.

2. Place your stiffened fabric headband on the table so that the webbing is visible (and not the printed cotton). Place the pattern in the centre and place the weight on top so that it does not move. Using a chalk hem marker, mark the outline of the card pattern on the adhesive webbing. Transfer all the markings: seam allowances and centre of the headband (centre front and centre back). Cut out the headband and make notches at your markings, with two snips of the scissors.

3. Fold the fabric over to the halfway point. Iron to flatten out the folds.

→ *Pin the ends to hold the fabric while you fold and iron.*

4. Place the headband on to the model and pin following the contours of the model. Decide on the width of your headband and fold under the fabric if necessary: at this stage, there is still time to make changes. Here, it is 5cm (2in) wide, which allows you to sew on the flowers easily. Try different positions for the flowers, then pin them in place. Tack the headband using normal thread or tacking thread (tacking is temporary sewing using wide stitches). Use a fine no. 7 Bohin couture needle or a DMC, which make a range of needles specially designed for millinery. Tack along the lengths of the headband: the front (forehead side) and the back (rear). Use sufficient thread to tack the two sides of the headband without having to make a knot or use extra thread. At the end, cut the thread and make a knot. Iron the headband to make sure that it is nice and flat.

5. Mark the seam allowance (1cm/½in) using chalk, on the inside of the headband and at the two ends. Fold over the seams of the headband.

→ *After folding, a little bit of fabric may be sticking out at the edges. Iron the seam flat again, and cut off the excess fabric diagonally across the corners. Leave 3mm of fabric at the corners, otherwise the headband may tear.*

Tack the ends of the headband (the shortest sides).

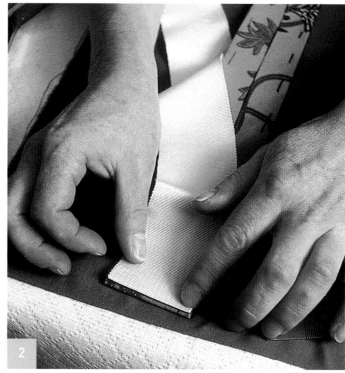

1 and 2. Mount the headband on some cotton grosgrain ribbon which is available in several widths; choose one in a width slightly smaller than that of the headband. Cut a piece of grosgrain to the length of the headband plus the seam allowance (here, 33cm/13in).

You can also use the grosgrain to decide the width of the headband.

→ *Grosgrain is a ribbon without a selvage and with a cotton weft, which means you can make it curl by ironing it with a steam iron. This process is known as 'curling grosgrain' or decatising.*

3. Fold the end of the grosgrain under and pin it along its length to the headband, placing the pins in the centre and leaving the edges that you are going to sew free.

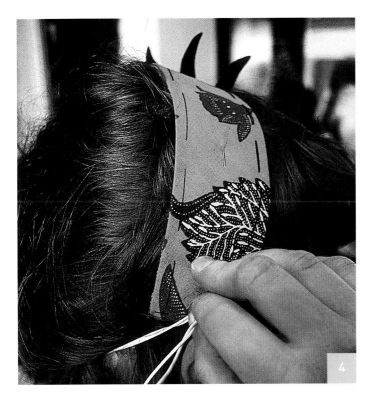

4 and 5. Take some hat elastic, which is cylindrical, and attach it to one end of the headband using a pin. Calculate the length around your head and double the elastic so that it holds better. It will be caught in when sewing the ends of the headband.

6. Tack the long and short sides.

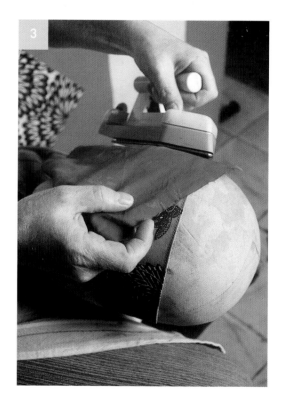

1. Move to the sewing machine. Set it up with cotton thread in a colour that matches the fabric; the spool thread should be matched to the colour of the grosgrain if this is not the same colour as the fabric.

Start sewing at the centre back of the headband. At the start, sew a finishing-off stitch, i.e. sew back and forth to prevent the thread from unravelling.

Sew in one go along one length and both the short sides of the headband. At the corners, turn before reaching the end of the headband. Do not sew along the second length; you will do this once you have sewn on the flowers. End with a finishing-off stitch.

2. Remove the tacking stitches using a stitch-unpicker.

3. Iron the headband on the model to get the right shape by placing a damp cloth between the iron and the headband to avoid making the fabric shiny. Here, Estelle is using a travel iron that is light and easy to use around the dolly. You can of course use a normal-sized iron.

Try on the headband in front of a mirror to check that it fits well.

4. On the dolly, place the flowers in position. You can follow the contour of the ear or make the flowers descend down the cheek. You can also slip a series of little flowers under the headband to make a fringe of petals all along the length.

Pin the flowers on to the headband in the chosen positions, and sew. Make tiny stitches using a matching thread and a fine needle, so that they are as invisible as possible. Without catching the grosgrain, sew the flowers to the fabric at their centre using a few tiny stitches. If the flowers are large, as here, attach them at several points in addition to the centre, still using invisible stitches. Sew the final length of the headband, taking care not to catch the petals in the sewing.

→ *If, by mistake, you have sewn all four sides of the headband in one go, sew the flower to the fabric taking care not to include the grosgrain, and finish off the thread by making the knot underneath the flower.*

ADDING GLITTER

Set off the crown by adding glitter to the centre and to the tips of the petals. Buy some glitter powder, for example the Swiss brand Glorex. It is available in all colours. Choose the shades according to those of the fabric.

➔ *You can also mix glitter of different shades to obtain a gradated look.*

1. Attach the glitter using colourless vinyl glue, which will not stain the fabric. Apply the glue with a delicate touch using a cotton bud (cut the cotton bud back if it is too large). Put a drop of glue on the ends of some of the petals and strips of glue elsewhere. Vary the motifs as you wish.

➔ *The glitter motif will be identical to the pattern made by the glue. If it is fine, the glitter will also be fine; if there is too much glue, this will result in rough patches of glitter.*

2. Once the glue has been applied, scatter the glitter on it immediately, using your fingers, a special glitter dispenser or by pouring it on directly.

Shake the model as you go to remove the excess glitter; this will show whether you have added sufficient glitter or not. If there is not enough glitter in some areas, add a bit more glue using a cotton bud and scatter more glitter.

➔ *Place a piece of paper beneath the model to catch the excess glitter and return it to the pot (to save money).*

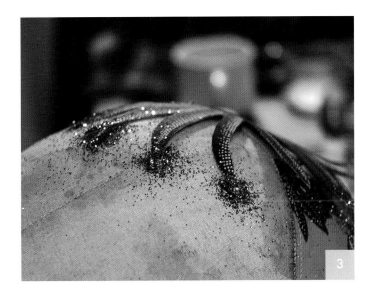

3

4

3 and 4. Estelle puts green glitter on the points of the red flower; pink glitter on the points of the blue flower; and two shades of pink mixed with white in the centre of the flowers.

Leave the crown to dry, without touching it, for 24 hours. Give the model a final shake. If you want to add more glitter, now is the time to do it; if not, then your crown is ready to wear. Why not wear some sparkly make-up to match?

→ *You can also decorate your headband with ready-made flowers that you have bought. For this, take some millinery flowers with flexible stems that can be bent under easily (in contrast to bouquets of flowers, where the metal stem is thick and inflexible).*

→ *If you want to make a crown from fresh flowers, choose species where the pistil will not stain the fabric of the headband. Choose flowers with a sturdy stem so that you can sew it to the headband – for example, lilies or orchids.*

→ *In winter, a leather, wool, tweed or synthetic fur headband would be more suitable. When working with these materials, use thread that is half cotton, half polyester; it is more flexible than cotton thread and is not likely to break when you sew through the various layers of fabric.*

Chinese-style cap

Originally, the cap was a military hat. At the end of the 19th century, it became the symbol of the working class. Its popularity was partly due to the proliferation of bicycles and cars – the visor protected cyclists and drivers from the sun. From 1930, milliners began to make the cap more feminine, and it took on various shapes: round, square or oblong. There were many models: Gavroche, Windsor, military, turf, jockey, etc. Here, Estelle invites you to make a very elegant Chinese-style cap, with a square visor, cut from toile de Jouy with a spring look. Toile de Jouy first appeared in the 18th century, when it was made by Christophe Philippe Oberkampf in a factory on the edge of the Bièvre river in Paris. There are numerous versions that rework the traditional motif and colours.

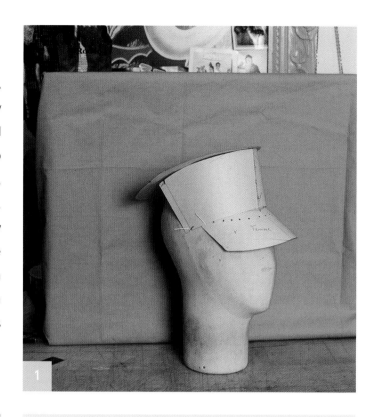

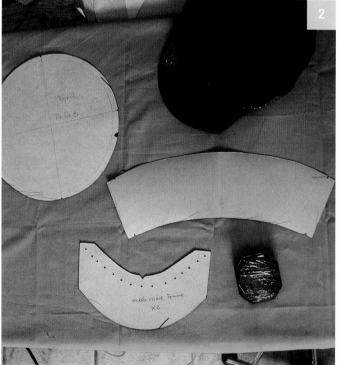

For a head circumference of 56cm (22in), choose a 60cm (23½in) square of fabric. For a head circumference of 60cm (23½in), choose a 75cm (29½in) square of fabric.

THE PATTERN

1 and 2. Cut out the pattern in pattern card. The cap is made up of a crown, two bands (front and back) and a visor.

→ *The pattern is based on a head circumference of 56cm (22in). This is the most common head circumference, as common as a size 5 shoe. The diameter of the crown is equal to 23.5cm (9¼in); each band forms half of the circumference of the circle (plus the seam allowances). Measure the circumference of your head using a tape measure and adjust the measurements above using the rule of three.*

THE VISOR

3. On the pattern for the visor, mark a line of regularly spaced points 1.5cm (½in) from the headline of the visor, then perforate the card at each point using a hole punch or a card punch. The perforations will serve as markers for matching the visor to the band. They mark a line that corresponds to the final hand-stitched topstitching that you will sew.

Place the pattern for the visor on the reverse of the well-ironed fabric. All the centre fronts of the pattern pieces must be on the bias of the fabric.

→ *If you are working with an animal motif, pay attention to the position of the drawings on the fabric (and later on the cap).*

Cut out two rectangles from toile de Jouy large enough for the pattern for the visor. The fabric will be stiffened by adhesive webbing, so cut out two rectangles of adhesive webbing the same size. Depending on the colouring of the toile de Jouy, choose either black or white adhesive webbing (it should not show through the fabric).

→ *For toile de Jouy, do not use adhesive webbing in Lycra. As the elasticity of the Lycra means that it is only suitable for stretchy fabrics.*

Attach the adhesive webbing to the two pieces of toile de Jouy, as you did before with the fabric for the crown of flowers.

→ *There are different thicknesses of adhesive webbing. Here, Estelle has selected a medium thickness of webbing, suitable for stiffening cotton fabric. You should choose a thickness of webbing (which will vary in flexibility) to match the degree of rigidity you want for your visor.*

4. Position the visor pattern on the stiffened toile de Jouy; mark the outline with a chalk hem marker and cut out. Remember to mark the perforated line using the chalk. Cut along the lines. Using the chalk, mark the notch located in the centre of the forehead, at the headline of the visor.

1 and 2. Lay the top and bottom of the visor together to check that they are identical.

Mark with a small notch the centre of the headline of the visor.

3. Iron again.

➔ *The more you iron, the more the adhesive webbing will stick.*

4. Move to the sewing machine to attach the top and bottom parts of the visor. Pin the two parts (right sides together) to prevent any slippage when sewing with the machine. The joining seam is the first visible topstitching on the visor. To topstitch this green fabric with burgundy motif, Estelle has chosen a burgundy thread in the same shade as the motif. You can also opt for a green thread. Whatever the colour, choose a thread of a similar shade or one shade darker or one shade lighter.

Place the presser foot at the edge of the visor so that you can follow its outline easily (the presser foot is the part of the sewing machine that passes over the fabric; it is made of two parallel branches between which the needle sews). When starting and finishing, sew a forward and a backstitch. N.B. Do not sew along the headline.

Turn the visor right side out and push out the corners using the point of a pair of scissors or a pencil, taking care not to pierce the fabric. Iron.

5. For the topstitching, start at the corners of the visor and at the edge. Start and finish each piece of topstitching with a forward and a backstitch.

At the 'corners', do not go right to the end, but turn beforehand (the width of the presser foot sets the distance between adjacent rows of topstitching). If you are not very experienced at sewing, practise by sewing on paper, cut out in the shape of the visor.

Make nine rows of topstitching, using the presser foot as a gauge for the spacing.

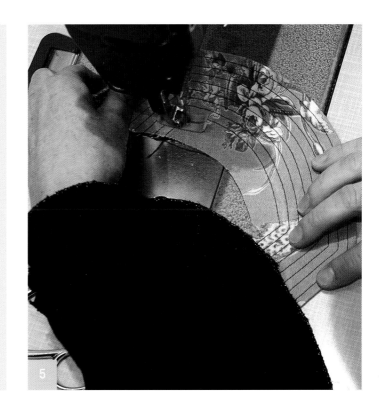

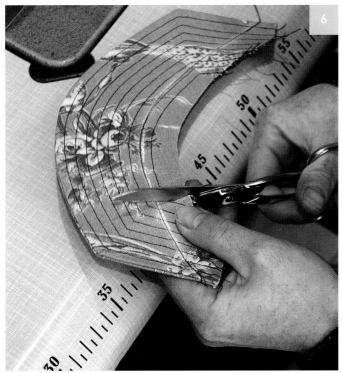

6. Measure 2cm (¾in) from the edge of the headline. Place pins along this line, then mark the line using chalk. This line will enable you to make notches in the visor, so that there is some flexibility around the headline.

Stitch along the line of chalk. With a pair of scissors, make notches every 2cm (¾in), from the edge to the line of sewing along the chalk marking.

The visor is now finished. Pin it to the model.

THE CROWN

1. On the toile de Jouy, mark the outlines of the patterns for the crown and the two bands using a chalk hem marker or a pencil (if the reverse of the fabric is light). Cut out. Mark the centre back and centre front points.

Pin the two bands right sides together.

2. Join the two bands using the sewing machine (still right sides together) by sewing the two short sides. Start and finish with a finishing-off stitch. Mark the centre of each band with a pencil.

3. Iron so that the seams are flat.

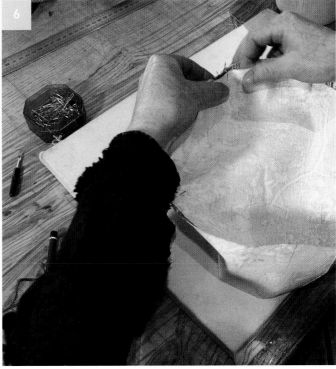

4. Using the sewing machine, sew two parallel lines of stitching, one either side of the seams already sewn, by placing the presser foot on the central seam and stitching on either side. Start and finish each row of stitching with a finishing-off stitch. Place the band on the model. If it is too high, you can still reduce it at this stage.

5. Fold the crown in two and check that the four marks around the edge match up exactly. If not, then mark them again.

6. Using pins, assemble the crown and the band, using the marks made with the pencil as a guideline. Make sure these marks line up and pin together. Use as many pins as possible to make the task easier.

Tack with tacking thread to make the join more secure. As Estelle has a lot of experience of this type of work, she is able to work with pins alone.

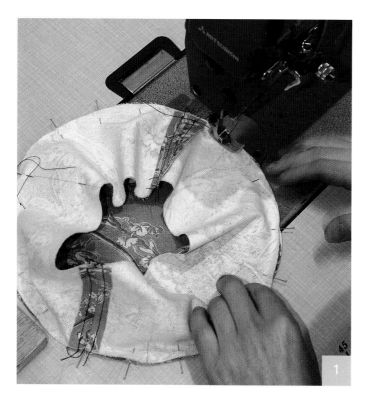

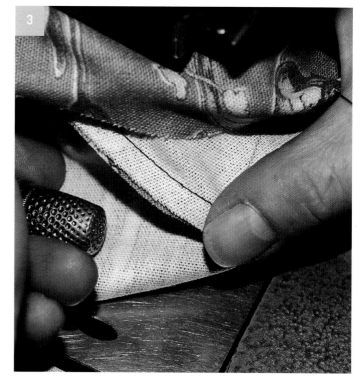

1. Sew using the sewing machine, lining up the presser foot parallel with the edge. Sewing in a circle requires some skill with the sewing machine. Again, you can practise beforehand on a piece of paper to avoid spoiling the fabric. Above all, take your time and sew slowly.

2 and 3. Remove all the pins apart from the one that indicates the centre front of the band.

Turn the fabric right side out. Topstitch by working on the right side of the fabric. As you sew, guide the seam allowances underneath using your thumb and index finger, folding them back towards the centre of the crown so that you sew over them.

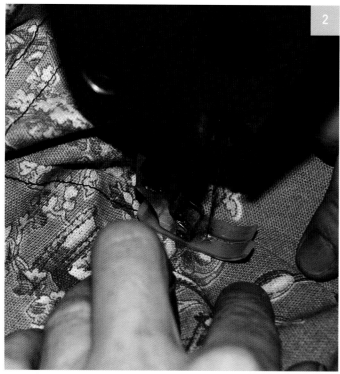

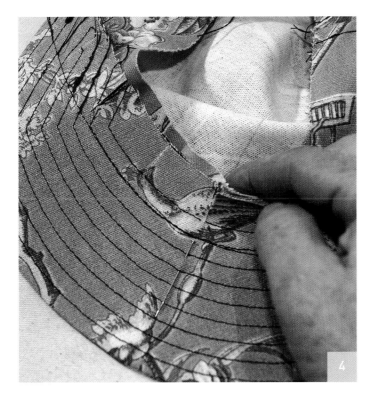

ASSEMBLING THE BAND AND THE VISOR

4. Join the visor and the band, right sides together and edge to edge, lining up the centre front of the visor with that of the band.

5. Pin, placing the pins perpendicular to the edge.

6. Tack along the line of topstitching that has been sewn 2cm (¾in) from the edge. Remove the pins, apart from the one that indicates the centre. Using the machine, sew the underneath of the visor over the tacking thread.

→ *Before sewing, make sure that the band lies smoothly against the visor.*

Iron again and remove the tacking thread using a stitch-unpicker.

THE TRIM

A decorative trim is placed over the visor to help mask the stem of the decorative flower.

1. Cut a band 3cm (1¼in) wide by 30cm (11¾in) long on the bias of the fabric.

Using an iron (without steam), stick on a 24cm (9½in) length of adhesive webbing, i.e. the length of the visor (22cm/8½in) plus a seam allowance of 1cm (½in) at each end. Stiffening the fabric will give it strength and prevent it from stretching.

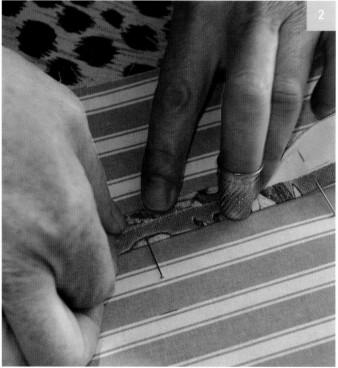

2. Mark the centre of the trim, lightly, using a pencil.

Turn under 5mm (¼in) of the stiffened fabric towards the inside. Pin the turned-under fabric, then turn the trim over to check that the edge is straight. Do the same thing for the other long side. Iron, tack along both lengths of turned-under fabric and remove the pins.

At one end, turn under 1.5cm (½in) of the fabric and iron again so that the trim is nice and flat.

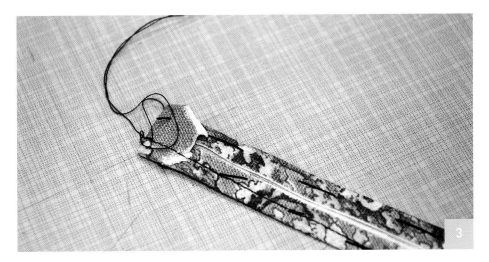

3. Sew using the machine so that you make two lines of stitching parallel to the edge. Sew on the right side of the fabric, placing one arm of the presser foot over the edge of the fabric (to prevent the two lines of sewing from being in the centre of the trim).

4. Pin the trim on the model, from one end to the other of the visor, so that you can adjust the length. Turn in the two ends and pin.

5. Using the sewing machine, sew the two ends by making the presser foot overlap the edge. The sewing must be 2–3mm (approx. ⅛in) from the end, which is the same as the width of one of the arms of the presser foot.

Remove the tacking using a stitch-unpicker.

→ *Put the trim to one side. You will sew it to the cap once the grosgrain is in place.*

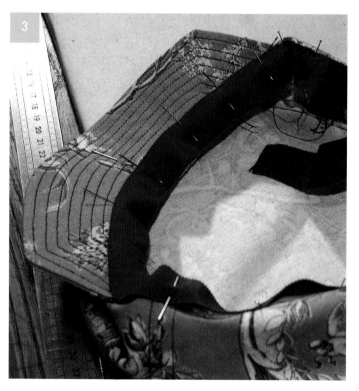

PLACING THE GROSGRAIN AROUND THE HEAD OPENING

1. Place the cap, inside out, on the model, lining up the centre back and centre front of the cap with the model. Using a pencil, mark the centre back and the centre front of the bands.

Choose a no. 5 grosgrain in a colour that goes with the fabric (here, bottle green grosgrain is used). For a head circumference of 56cm (22in), take 58cm (23in) of grosgrain, i.e. the head circumference plus 1cm (½in) seam allowance at each end.

2. Pin the grosgrain to the band. At each end of the grosgrain, turn under 1cm (½in) – equivalent to the seam allowances – and secure the turning with a pin. Pin the grosgrain from the centre back of the band, aligning the mid-line with the edge of the band, so that it can then be turned under inside the cap. This process will take a long time for a novice – be patient.

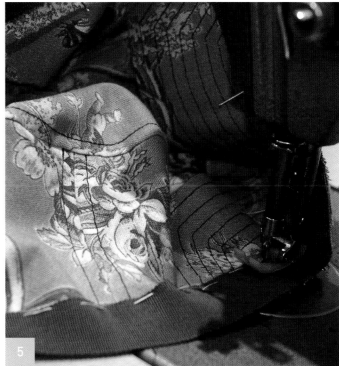

3. At the visor, attach the edge of the grosgrain to the notched sewing line (and not to the topstitching).

4. Tack the grosgrain. Remove the pins.

5 and 6. Sew using the machine with a thread that matches the grosgrain (here, khaki green thread is used). Place the presser foot so that it overlaps the grosgrain. You need to sew on the edge in order to include the 'teeth' of the grosgrain (i.e. the loops at the edge of the grosgrain) in the sewing.

Remove the tacking thread.

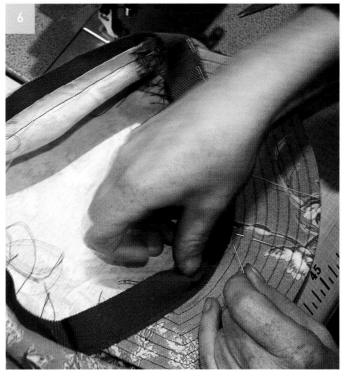

ATTACHING THE TRIM AND THE FLOWER

All that remains now to finish the hat is to make the lining. Before doing that, you need to sew on the trim and attach the flower, as once the lining is in place, you will no longer have access to the interior of the cap.

1. Place the cap on the model and attach the trim by pinning the ends. The trim is sewn on by hand. Use the burgundy thread previously used for the topstitching. Use the thread double.

Sew the two ends of the trim. To start, sew from underneath and bring the needle out at a place where the machine stitching crosses. You need to sew on the previous lines of sewing and topstitching, so that your sewing is invisible. Finish off the thread with a knot. Attach the other end of the trim in the same way.

Iron the cap on the model, stopping just as you reach the level of the grosgrain. Gently iron again using steam.

→ *N.B. Toile de Jouy is a durable cotton. You can therefore iron over it without risk. If you are making a cap in wool, silk or lamé, use a damp cloth to prevent these more fragile fabrics from damage.*

2. Take a millinery flower with a stem made from fine millinery wire, which is easy to sew, bend and hide. Wrap the flower stem around the end of the trim and sew it on to the band using a few stitches and a green cabled thread, which is very thick and made up of several threads. You can also use an embroidery thread.

→ *N.B. Do not sew the flower either to the grosgrain or to the trim!*

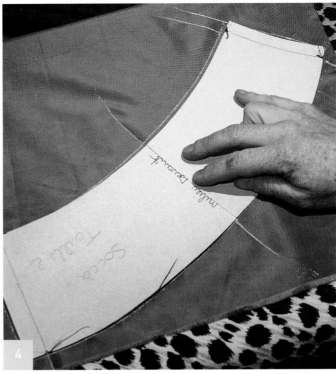

THE LINING

For the lining, choose some cotton or silk fabric. Do not use synthetic fabric (otherwise you will perspire). Here, Estelle uses a grey/pink taffeta, the colour of which changes depending on the light. Iron the fabric well.

3 and 4. Use the patterns for cutting out the crown and the bands in toile de Jouy. Proceed as before: on the bias of the lining, mark the crown and the two bands using chalk. Mark the centre back and centre front points using the chalk, cut out and iron again.

5. Pin the two bands together. Sew the short sides by machine to make the band for the lining, in the same way as you previously joined the bands in the toile de Jouy. Choose a thread one shade darker or one shade lighter. This slight difference will create a prettier effect than if you were to use a thread in exactly the same colour.

Open the seam allowances and iron the turnings nice and flat. Return to the machine and make two lines of stitching either side of the joining seam that you have just sewn.

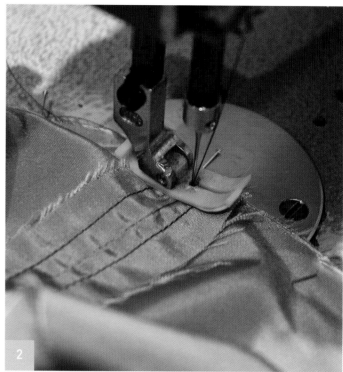

1. Assemble the crown and the bands, right sides together, using pins. If the fabric selected does not have a wrong or a right side, the wrong side of the bands is the side on to which the seam allowances have been turned back.

2. Sew by placing the presser foot on the edge of the band. Sew slowly, carefully following the curve of the band. Use the burgundy thread used for the topstitching.

3. Slip the lining into the inside of the hat, lining up the seams of the taffeta bands with those of the toile de Jouy bands.

4. Turn down the taffeta towards the inside with a seam allowance of 1cm (⅜in). Pin on to the toile de Jouy 2mm (⅛in) from the grosgrain.

→ N.B. When pinning, do not pass through the toile de Jouy. Do not catch either the right side of the toile de Jouy or the grosgrain.

Take some old rose sewing thread and use it double.

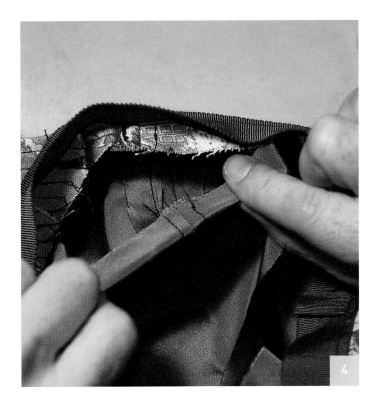

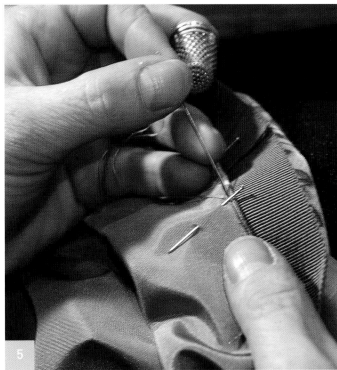

5. Sew by hand, starting under the taffeta. Pick up a loop of toile de Jouy and come out just above the taffeta. Sew a hem that does not pass through the toile de Jouy, catching in one tooth in every three at the edge of the grosgrain.

6. When you come to the visor, do not pass through it. With the needle, catch a little fabric from beneath the visor, and sew only a few, tiny stitches inside the cap.

To finish, turn the grosgrain inside the cap so that it is invisible from the outside. Iron lightly, and the cap is finished!

→ *If you like glitter, you could add glitter to the top of the cap, as was done with the crown of flowers.*

→ *You can make caps in various styles, depending on the fabric you use: woollen fabric will make the cap into a winter one; lamé will make it into something very chic.*

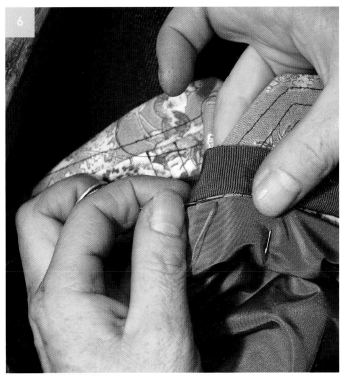

Beret

There are several types of beret in various sizes, from the ample, velvet faluche worn by Rembrandt to the traditional Basque beret (in fact, this beret is of Béarnaise origin, but the Basques integrated the hat belonging to their neighbours from Béarn into their national costume a long time ago). Here, Estelle has made a hat comprising a crown, two bands and a headband, which gives the beret added style.

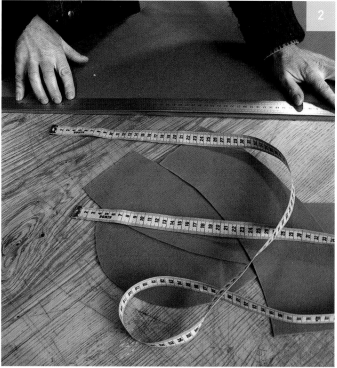

THE PATTERN

1. Use the same pattern for the crown and bands as for the Chinese-style cap. Mark the patterns using a chalk hem marker on the bias of the fabric (a pure new wool fabric). Cut out.

➜ *Remove the traces of chalk on the fabric using a nailbrush (dry).*

THE HEADBAND

2. For the headband, mark a band 7cm (2¾in) wide and 70cm (27½in) long on the bias of the fabric. Cut out, then mark the centre with a chalk line. Leave a 1cm (½in) seam allowance at each end of the strip.

3 and 4. To structure the head opening, reinforce the headband with a no. 5 grosgrain (2.5cm/1in wide). Cut 70cm (27½in) of grosgrain (the colour does not really matter, as it will be hidden inside the folded up fabric).

Place the edge of the grosgrain in the centre of the band. Pin and tack the grosgrain along the centre line of the strip.

5. Join the two ends of the strip, securing it with two pins placed along the seam allowances.

6. Sew by machine to close up the two ends of the strip, starting and finishing with a finishing-off stitch.
Sew two lines of stitching, one on either side of the first line of sewing.

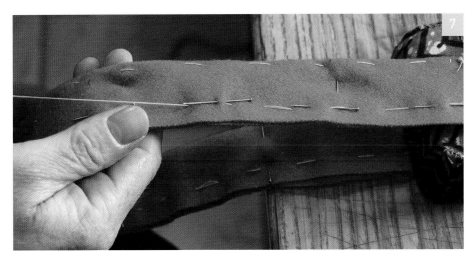

7. Fold the fabric lengthwise over the grosgrain (the grosgrain has been tacked, so it will not move).

Pin; the fold of the fabric must run exactly along the edge of the grosgrain. When finished, the headband should have a width of 2.5cm (1in), equal to that of the grosgrain.

THE BANDS

1. Pin the two bands together. Try out the bands (inside out) against the headband.

Pin the headband at 2.5cm (1in), i.e. the same as the width of the grosgrain. Tack and remove the pins.

Iron to make sure that the turn-up is nice and flat, using a protective cloth to avoid spoiling the pure new wool fabric. Use scissors to cut off any excess.

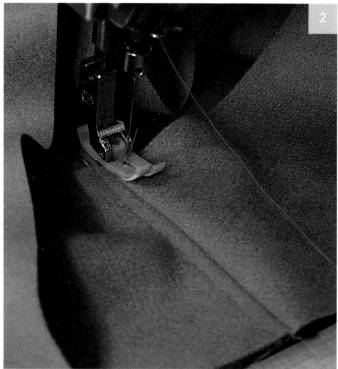

2. Using the machine, join the two bands at each end. Sew at the seam allowance (1cm/½in). Start and finish with a finishing-off stitch.

Sew two rows of stitching, one either side of this joining seam, starting and finishing with a finishing-off stitch.

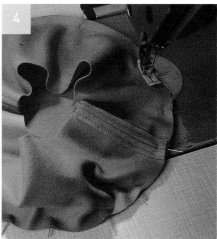

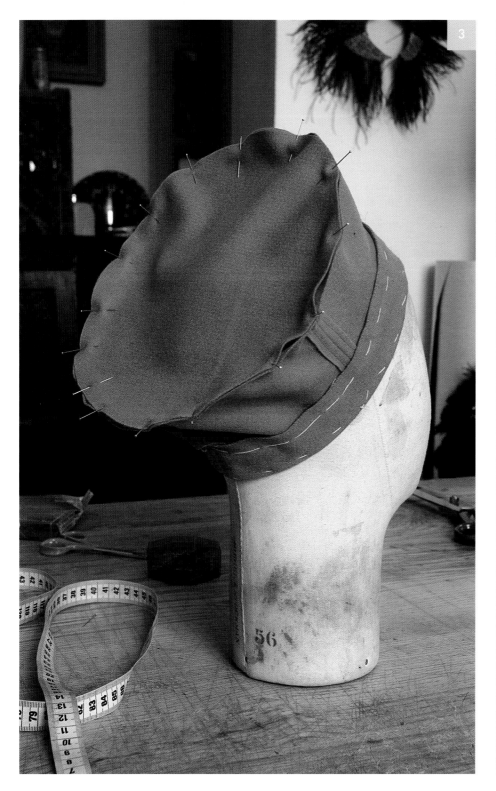

THE CROWN

3. Pin the bands to the crown. Start with four pins at the four main points of the hat – centre back, centre front, centre right and centre left – then pin in between these four points.

Tack 1cm (½in) away from the edge.

4. Using the machine, sew along the line of tacking, 1cm (½in) away from the edge.

Once the joining seam has been sewn, turn the seam allowances up inside the beret. Do not open them, leave them together, then turn them up towards the inside and sew. This is how you are able to topstitch the crown.

➔ *The topstitching is done with an orange thread.*

ATTACHING THE HEADBAND TO THE CROWN

Using pins, mark the centre front of your headband and line it up with the centre front of the band (inside out). Place the band and the headband edge to edge and then pin. Do an initial fitting with the pins.

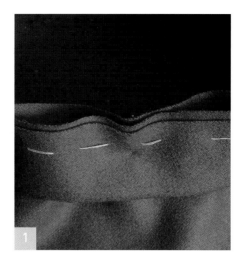

1. Tack and remove the pins.

2. Sew by following the tacking thread on the headband: sew slowly, holding the woollen fabric taut. Take care that the volume of fabric at the edges of the band and the headband does not cause folds to form whilst you are sewing.

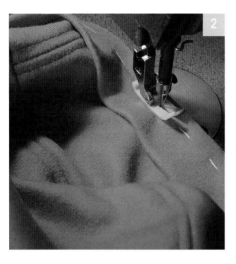

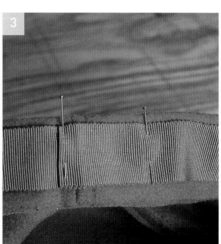

PLACING THE GROSGRAIN AROUND THE HEAD OPENING

3. Choose a no. 5 grosgrain in pink (to match your fabric). Fit it, starting at the centre back. Fold the grosgrain under at the start and at the finish. Pin as you go along.

4 and 5. Sew the grosgrain by hand. Start at the centre back, underneath the grosgrain. Pick up a little of the woollen fabric and a tooth of the grosgrain. Take care not to go through to the front of the woollen fabric. Continue with hem stitch, picking up one tooth in every three of the grosgrain. At the end, this sewing should be invisible.

→ *The grosgrain will maintain the shape of the head opening. It will also absorb perspiration. Some of your foundation may come off on the grosgrain around the head opening. From time to time, clean it with a damp cloth soaked in a little surgical spirit.*

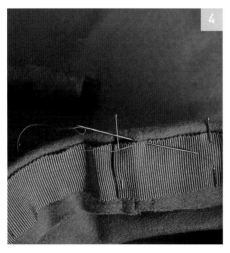

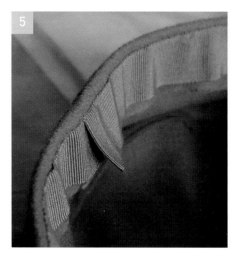

THE LINING

Proceed as with the lining for the Chinese-style cap. Iron the cotton or silk lining. Here, Estelle is using an orange silk with a shimmering effect. Use the patterns for the crown and the bands. Working on the bias, transfer the patterns for the crown and the bands with a chalk hem marker. Cut out the silk with a pair of dressmaking scissors.

6. Put the two bands together as done previously for the woollen bands. Sew a joining seam at each end, then sew two lines of stitching, one on either side of this joining seam. Estelle sewed the pink woollen fabric with orange thread and the orange lining with pink thread. Line up the crown and the bands as you did earlier with the woollen fabric. Spread the crown fabric evenly around the circumference of the hat and pin. Start by pinning the four main points of the beret, then place a pin every centimetre. Tack and remove the pins as you go. If you are happy using the sewing machine, you can sew directly after pinning, without tacking. Sew slowly, following the edge with the presser foot. Start and finish with a finishing-off stitch.

Topstitch by overlapping the previous sewing with the presser foot.

7. Fit the lining into the beret by lining up the seams of the bands in the woollen fabric with those of the silk fabric.

Turn up the grosgrain at the headline. Turn down the edge of the lining as far as the seam joining the headband and bands of the beret. Pin the lining and bands together at the seams. Pin throughout.

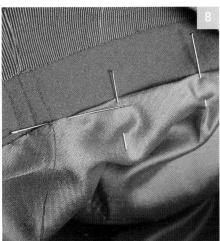

8. Sew by hand. Take a long milliner's needle, and some orange thread. Start at the side, at one of the joining seams for the bands, under the lining. On the joining seam for the headband and the band, take up a little of the woollen fabric with the point of the needle (without passing through the fabric), and then sew through the silk. Continue with hem stitch approx. 1cm (½in) in size.

Finish off the thread with a knot concealed beneath the lining. Turn down the pink grosgrain and the beret is finished.

→ *You can also make a beret from leather, suede or cotton, or even change the style of the beret by removing the headband. This would mean that the beret would just consist of a crown and two bands. You could add a trim at the front, identical to the one for the Chinese-style cap.*

Bibi

The word 'bibi' appeared in the 19th century, during the Second French Empire, to describe a little bonnet worn by elegant romantics. Later, the word was used to describe a miniature hat that was perched, rather than fitted, on the head. The bibi is kept in place with the use of hair pins or a piece of elastic. During the 1940s, it took the shape of a pillbox or a *chapeau de singe*.

To make one of these elegant little decorative pieces, without too much difficulty, Estelle suggests that you buy a tambourine hat frame from Artnuptia (or any specialist millinery supplier). The hat frame is made from double webbing, stiffened and edged with a piano string. The fabric you use to cover the hat frame will set the style of the bibi. You can choose the fabric so that your bibi matches a particular outfit. You can also cover the tambourine with flowers, sewing the stems and sticking the underneath of the petals directly on to the hat frame, which you cover completely. You could also hide the tambourine beneath shells, sewn next to each other, adding glue in the gaps, and then scattering with sand. Here, Estelle has chosen to cover the tambourine with a woollen fabric.

THE CROWN

1. It is not possible to attach the fabric directly to the hat frame. You need to attach it to a support, such as the flannelette used here. Edge the inside of the tambourine with some flannelette by cutting out a strip 60cm (23½in) long by 4cm (1½in) wide on the bias. Pin it to the hat frame with four pins and sew the flannelette using a long stitch (the stitches will not be visible at the end).

→ *N.B. If your fabric is light, use white flannelette so that it does not show through.*

Leave the flannelette head opening open. You will sew it later with the fabric, for which it will serve as a guide.

In a mirror, choose the position of the tambourine on your head (tilted forward or to one side). Once you have made your choice, place the tambourine on the dolly in the same way and mark the four centres (centre front, centre back, centre right and centre left) with a pin. Mark these points with a pencil inside the hat frame, remove the pins and iron the fabric.

2 and 3. A crown tip and a band are needed to cover the tambourine. For a head circumference of 58cm (22¾in), make an oval crown tip by marking the ends of a 21 × 18cm (8¼in × 7in) cross and then joining up the marks. Draw the outline of the crown tip on the bias of the fabric and cut out, leaving a 1cm (½in) seam allowance all round.

4. Pin the crown tip to the hat frame with fine pins. Start by placing pins in the four centres (centre back, centre front, centre right and centre left), then add pins between these four points. Whilst pinning, smooth the fabric and pull it out to avoid folds.

Sew the fabric crown tip to the hat frame using backstitch (which will be hidden beneath the band); use the thread double and start at the centre back. Sew from the inside of the hat towards the outside taking in the tambourine and the fabric. From the second stitch, sew a backstitch. Pass the needle from the inside to the outside and then go back through. Hold the fabric using your thumb. To finish off, make a knot on the inside of the hat frame. Remove the pins. Cut off the excess fabric to avoid too much bulk. Cut along the sewing line, making sure you do not cut into it.

1. Cut out a 12cm (4¾in) wide band on the bias of the fabric, making the length the same as the circumference of the hat, here 70cm (27½in). Iron.

Fold under the edge of the band and place it around the hat frame, being careful to avoid folds. Pin the two ends at the centre back and cut off the excess fabric.

2. Close up the band by sewing with the sewing machine. Slip the band on to the crown. Pin by folding the upper edge of the band inside by 1cm (½in); use a small, flat ruler to help you make the turning all around the crown tip.

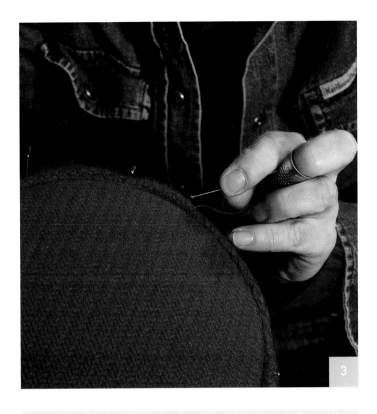

3. Remove the tambourine from the dolly and sew the band to the crown tip, using red thread and small stitches. Start at the centre back. Sew from the inside of the hat towards the outside, taking in the hat frame, flannelette and fabric with each stitch; sew with a simple straight stitch. Remove the pins as you go. Finish off by tying the thread in a knot, beneath the flannelette, at the centre back.

4 and 5. Fold the woollen fabric inside the tambourine by 1cm (½in), then sew it to the inside of the hat frame, without passing the thread through to the outside.

THE DECORATION

Cut out a piece of woollen fabric on the bias, 20cm (36¼in) wide by 92cm (7¾in) long, and stiffen it with some adhesive webbing. Fold the fabric in two to make it into a kind of cravat for the decoration. Cut the two ends on a slant.

1. Fold the fabric in two to find the mid-way point. Mark it with chalk, then make two other chalk marks 8cm (3¼in) either side of the centre. When you are sewing, you must leave this 16cm (6½in) gap open (unsewn) so that the fabric can be turned inside out later.

Pin the two pieces of fabric right sides together. Partially close up the seams by sewing on the machine using red thread. Start at one of the points, with a finishing-off stitch. Sew up to the first mark drawn in chalk and sew a finishing-off stitch. Start off again with a finishing-off stitch at the third chalk mark, 16 cm (6½ in) further on, and sew as far as the other point.

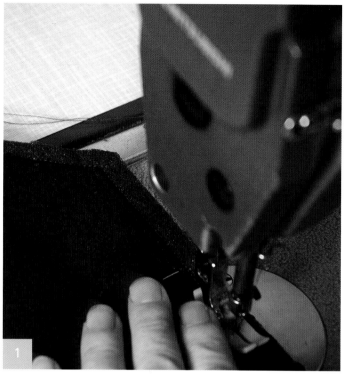

Finish off your thread with a finishing-off stitch. Once sewn, remove the excess fabric along the line of sewing (to avoid too much bulk when you turn the band right-side out). When you reach the opening, stop cutting, retain the excess fabric for the length of the opening and start cutting again on the other side of the 16cm (6½in) opening. Iron.

2. Turn the decoration the right way out. With this thick, woollen fabric, it can be a little difficult to turn the piece. Take your time. Slip the point of a wooden stick or the end of a paintbrush inside the decoration to push out the points. Iron on the right side, ironing down the edges (place a protective cloth over the fabric to prevent damage to the wool).

3. Pinch the decoration together to form pleats (this will determine the length of the tails of the decoration). Fold over the loop to form a rose.

1. Pin the decoration into shape on the hat. You will want to try several ways before you find the ideal place for it. Undo the loop and sew the pleats. Attach the decoration using stitches hidden beneath the knot. Sew through the hat, except where you might see the stitches; in those cases, do not sew through the entire thickness of the hat. Use tiny stitches by taking up just one fibre of the woollen fabric. As this woollen fabric is thick, it is easy to conceal the stitching. When you have finished, you should have the impression that the knot is holding itself.

2. Pin the grosgrain at the headline, starting at the centre back. Take 40cm (15¾in) of hat elastic and cut it in four, then make four loops that you sew in at the same time as the grosgrain. This elastic, held in place by hair pins, will enable you to keep the tambourine on your head.

➜ *Choose black elastic if you have brown hair and white elastic if you are blonde, so that it can be hidden in your hair. Soften the white of the elastic with a little foundation to make it into a light beige.*

Slip the elastic loops beneath the grosgrain at the four main points of the hat: centre front, centre back, centre right and centre left.

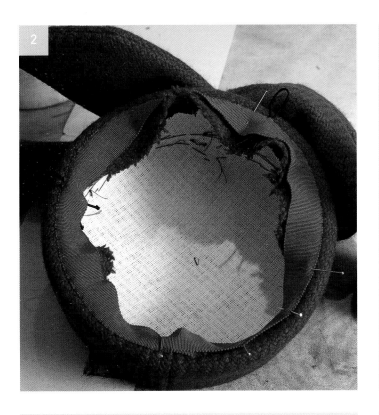

Sew the grosgrain by hand, attaching the elastic as you go. Use the thread double, in a colour that matches the grosgrain, and start to sew at the centre back. Push the needle under the grosgrain and catch the flannelette, the fabric and one tooth of the grosgrain. Sew a stitch every three teeth.

THE LINING

3. Cut out a pattern smaller than the one you used for the woollen crown tip and band. For the crown tip, cut out an oval pattern, the exact size of the crown tip of the tambourine. Cut out a band 12cm (4¾in) wide, and equal in length to the internal circumference of the tambourine, measured with a tape measure, to which you have added a 2cm (¾in) seam allowance. Iron the lining fabric and place the patterns on the bias of the fabric. Transfer the patterns using a chalk hem marker and cut out.

Using the sewing machine, close up the band with a row of stitching. Sew two lines of stitching, one either side of the closing seam.

Join together the crown tip and the band by pinning and sewing, as you did previously for the cap and beret. To make pinning the circumference easier and to hold the lining, put the first pin on the crown tip. Sew the lining to the grosgrain, then turn the lining back inside. Pin the wrong side to the grosgrain and attach the lining with a slip stitch.

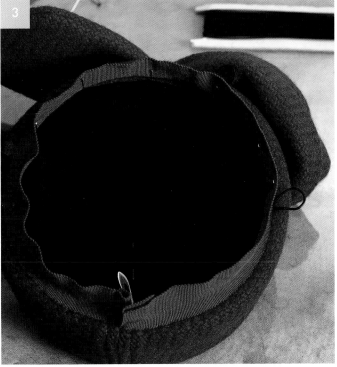

Wide-brimmed hat

A caricature published in 1857 showed a bourgeois addressing his servant, 'Baptiste, where is Madame?' – 'Over there, Monsieur, under her hat.' The wide-brimmed hat was introduced at the end of the 18th century, giving way to the bonnet by 1860. During the second half of the 19th century, it re-emerged. During the Belle Époque, it triumphed. Nowadays, the wide-brimmed hat is still fashionable, whether made from straw, felt, velvet, vinyl or padded silk like the one Estelle suggests you make here.

THE PATTERN

1. Draw the crown on to pattern card. For a head circumference of 58cm (22¾in), trace a 21 × 18cm (8¼ × 7in) cross and make an oval by joining up the ends of the two straight lines. Draw one half and then fold the card so that the two sides are identical. This pattern for the crown tip of the hat is the same as the head opening of the wide-brimmed hat.

Use sticky tape to attach a sheet of pattern card to your desk. Place the pattern for the crown tip in the middle of the sheet and reproduce it on the large sheet.

Using the oval crown tip, draw the brim of the hat, 13cm (5in) wide. You can use a special ellipse drawing instrument to help you draw the curves if you have one; otherwise, mark points 13cm (5in) from the edge of the crown tip using a ruler, then join up these points using a pencil.

1

THE CROWN TIP

2 and 3. Cut out the outline of the brim with a pair of scissors and remove the centre using a cutter by drawing lines radiating from the centre and running the cutter along these lines; finish by cutting out each segment with the scissors.

4. Using a pencil, draw the marks for the centres: centre front and centre side. Place the centre front of the pattern on the line of the bias and cut out the silk on the bias. Cut out two squares of silk for the brim (top and underneath).

5 and 6. Stiffen the silk brims with adhesive webbing. Cut two squares of webbing on the bias the same size as the silk squares. As the silk is fairly light in colour, Estelle is using a white webbing so that it is not visible through the fabric. Pin the silk to the adhesive webbing and stick them together by ironing with a very hot iron (maximum temperature) without steam. Iron on the side of the webbing and not the silk to avoid folds or bubbling and to prevent the fabric from yellowing. Iron slowly to ensure that the silk is well glued. Place the pattern for the brim of the hat on to the webbing of one of the glued squares. Draw around the outline and the head opening using a pencil. Mark the ends of the lines radiating from the centre. Cut off the excess fabric.

1. To remove the head opening, fold the fabric in half and cut out, leaving a 2.5cm (1in) margin around the head opening. This will give you the seam allowance and a safety margin that will enable you to reduce the size of the head opening if it is a little too big.

Repeat this operation on the other piece of glued fabric. Iron the fabric once more.

2. Place the two hat brims on top of one another, right sides together. Line the markings up exactly using pins: the centre front of the first piece with the centre front of the second piece, then the centre backs and the centre sides in the same way.

Smooth out the fabric and iron carefully. Put four pins around the brims to ensure that the fabric does not move while you are sewing.

→ *If there is a little discrepancy between the two pieces, do not worry as you can correct it on the machine, basing your stitching on the smallest piece.*

Choose an orange thread, in a matching shade, to join the top and the underneath of the brim of the hat by machine. Sew slowly and carefully, gradually turning the fabric as you go. The seam allowance here is equal to the width of the presser foot, parallel to the outside edge.

3. Iron both sides again. Remove the pins and turn the fabric the right way out. Pull it out well. Use the end of your finger to trace along the seam on the inside. Pinch around the edge and shake to even out the seam. Iron by opening the seam, without steam, being very careful not to burn the silk: iron quickly, without letting the iron rest in any particular place.

4. On the machine, stitch a series of parallel lines of topstitching around the joined brims. This stitching has an aesthetic effect and also makes the brim of the hat more flexible.

Mark the centre with pins. Start and finish each row of topstitching where you have placed the centre pins. All the knots will be at this spot. Check that the spool is full of thread (orange, the same as before): you are going to need a lot of thread and you do not want to have to change the spool while topstitching.

Start and finish with a forward and finishing-off stitch. Cut the thread at the end of each row of topstitching. The lines of topstitching must be concentric and spaced half a presser-foot width apart.

→ *When the first two rows of topstitching have been done, iron nice and flat. Do not iron backwards and forwards, but iron from the outside of the brim towards the centre opening. Iron again after completing another two or three rows of topstitching.*

Once all the topstitching has been done, iron again (from the centre towards the outside edge), then cut off the threads of the finishing-off stitches you made at the start and finish of each row of topstitching.

5. Cut notches around the head opening as far as the first row of topstitching, every 2cm (¾in), being careful not to cut the thread of the topstitching.

6. Try out on the dolly or on your head. If it is too small, cut the notches a little further, beyond the first row of stitching. Place a pin in the centre front.

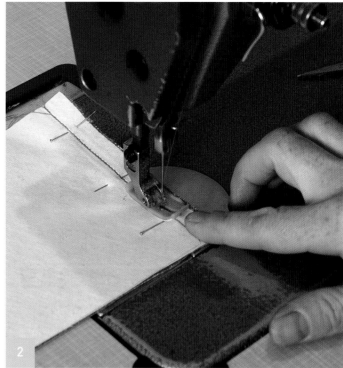

THE CROWN

1. Cut the crown tip and the band from the silk to form the crown of the hat. The band measures 58cm (22¾in) long by 12cm (4¾in) wide. The 58cm (22¾in) corresponds to the circumference of the head. The 12cm (4¾in) includes the seam allowances (approx. 1cm/½in). Cut the silk to the pattern measurements (the seam allowance is included in the pattern). Draw the centre with a pencil, as well as the 1cm (½in) seam allowance at each end.

2. Pin right sides together, tack and sew along the line drawn 1cm (½in) from the two ends.
Open out the seams with the iron.

3. Using the machine, make two rows of stitching, one to the left and one to the right of the seam.
Place the band on the dolly to get an idea of the final effect. If it is too tall, cut it down.

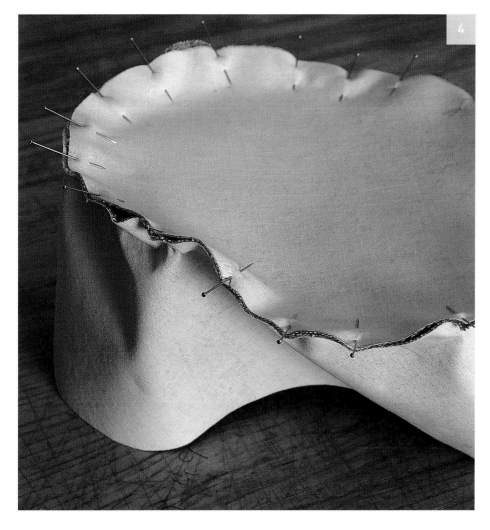

4. Attach the oval crown tip to the band using the marks made in pencil as a guide. Line up the marks, and pin. Spread the fabric evenly around the circumference of the hat, even if it means moving the pins slightly from their markings. The more pins you use, the better your work will be held.

Tack, then sew by machine. Sew in a circle, holding the fabric firmly and keep checking that there are no folds, either underneath or on top.

→ *If, once you have finished, you notice that there is a fold in spite of the care you have taken, unpick the sewing for 2cm (¾in) with a stitch-unpicker and sew again until you get the perfect result.*

5. Turn the crown out and iron the band on the reverse to avoid damaging the fabric. Place a pressing cushion inside and iron gently over the sewing for the crown tip and the band.

6. Turn the crown inside out again. Open the seam allowances with the point of the iron, then make notches in the seam allowances every centimetre (½in) with the point of a pair of scissors.

→ *To avoid cutting the band when making the notches, hold your index finger under the blade of the scissors to help control where you cut.*

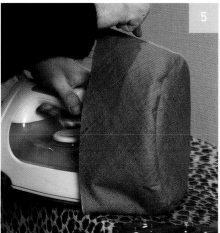

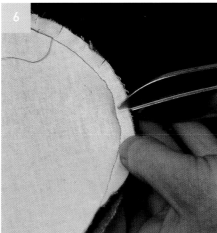

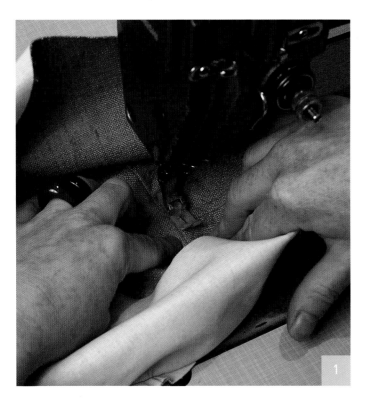

1 and 2. Secure the seam allowances by sewing two parallel lines, one either side of the seam. The seam allowance for the crown tip will be sewn on to the crown tip and the seam allowance for the band will be sewn on to the band. It is very important, and you must check as you go along, that the seam allowances for the crown tip and the band are well separated. When you have finished, turn the crown right side out and iron the inside again.

3. Pin the crown to the head opening in the brim to try it out, placing the pins parallel to the edge of the head opening. Try on the hat and check the height of the crown. If the head opening is a little small in relation to the crown, make the notches you have already made larger with scissors.

ATTACHING THE GROSGRAIN AROUND THE HEAD OPENING

4. Cut 60cm (23½in) of grosgrain 2.5cm (1in) wide, then pin it following the notching and the last line of topstitching on the brim of the hat. When finished, the top of the grosgrain should form a perfect oval.

5. Tack the grosgrain before sewing by machine. In haute couture, the grosgrain around the head opening would be sewn by hand, but, to make it simple for you, Estelle suggests you do this by machine. Sew around the edge of the grosgrain so that you only catch the loops of the edging.

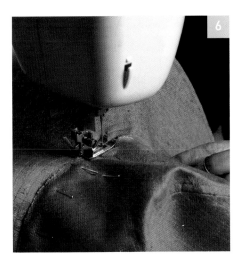

ASSEMBLING THE CROWN AND THE BRIM

6. Place the crown and the brim on the dolly. Pin, starting at the centre front, then centre back and centre sides. Sew by hand, using the thread double, or sew on the machine, placing it on the edge of the table, so that you can turn the hat. Before sewing, move the grosgrain away from the head opening so that it is not included in the sewing, which will be hidden beneath a decorative grosgrain ribbon.

Once the crown is attached to the brim, place the hat on the dolly and iron the part that you have just sewn lightly, using steam to flatten out the edging well.

THE DECORATION

1. Take 60cm (23½in) of no. 9 grosgrain (4cm/1½in wide) in orange. The 60cm (23½in) corresponds to a 58cm (23½in) head circumference and a 2cm (¾in) seam allowance. Try out several ways of placing this wide, decorative grosgrain around the crown.

2 and 3. Using a pin, close up the orange grosgrain at the centre right side. Turn the seam allowances of the grosgrain inside, at the two ends, and pin without catching the black grosgrain around the head opening inside the crown.
Sew the grosgrain by hand. Start by closing up the ends of the grosgrain by sewing it from top to bottom. Use small stitches, pushing the needle through from the inside of the hat to the outside, avoiding catching the black grosgrain around the head opening. Finish by knotting the thread inside the crown.

Attach the orange grosgrain with a stitch in the centre front, a stitch in the centre back and a stitch in the centre side opposite the side you have just sewn. These stitches should be invisible. Do this by pushing the needle through from the inside and bringing it out through a tooth of the grosgrain. Pass the needle back into the crown and finish off the thread on the inside of the crown. When making the knot, do not pull too hard on the thread, as the invisibility of the stitch also depends upon the tension of the thread: a thread that is pulled too hard will create a mark indicating the presence of a stitch.

4. Make a flat bow that you will attach to the grosgrain. To make this bow, take a piece of grosgrain 30cm (12in) long and bring the two ends to the centre, overlapping by 1cm (½in) at each end. Iron the folded grosgrain.

→ *Always use steam when ironing the grosgrain, using a damp cloth, otherwise the ironing will make it shiny.*

Pin the closure of the grosgrain and sew by hand with straight stitch by following the visible edging of the grosgrain and by taking in all the layers of the grosgrain with each stitch. Cut another piece of grosgrain, 10cm (4in) long this time, and place it crossways in the centre of the grosgrain that you have just sewn. Fold this second piece of grosgrain around the first and fold the edge under. Pin and sew by hand using straight stitch, without catching the grosgrain below; do not pull the thread too much, otherwise you risk puckering the grosgrain and making a bow tie rather than a flat bow.

1 and 2. Take a long piece of grosgrain to make the tails of the bow that will hang over the edge of the hat. Place the grosgrain at an angle on the brim and find the position that you like best. Once you have found it, pin the tails on to the grosgrain on the crown and on to the brim, folding the ends under to hide them, then cut. On the brim, the grosgrain must be cut on a slant to follow the line of the edge of the hat. Sew the tails on to the grosgrain on the crown.

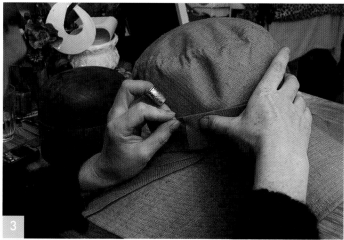

3. Sew the bow to the hat with four invisible stitches at the four corners by slipping the needle inside the folded part of the bow and bringing it out, taking in the grosgrain underneath at the same time, then insert it back into the bow and finish off the thread with a knot. You need to give the impression that the bow is holding itself.

Place the hat on to the model.

Iron the two tails of grosgrain, placing a towel or damp cloth between the grosgrain and the iron to prevent the grosgrain from becoming shiny.

4. Sew an invisible stitch to attach the tail of the grosgrain that is not being held by the bow (at the base of the crown).

5. Using invisible stitches, sew the ends of the turned-under tails to the brim of the hat, as described above. Sew four stitches at each end.

→ *Sewing the decorative grosgrain was one of the first things that Christiane and Marinette taught Estelle during her apprenticeship. According to these two professionals, someone who does not know how to sew decorative grosgrain in such a way that the ribbon gives the impression of holding itself, without having been sewn, cannot be a milliner.*

Finish making the wide-brimmed hat by making a lining from the pattern you used to make the crown from padded silk. Making and fitting the lining are identical to the process used for the Chinese-style cap (see pages 57–58). The delicate (and long) process of fitting the lining takes place when you sew the padded silk to the grosgrain.

Sew by hand using a normal needle. Start (and finish) at the centre back. Catch some fibres from the padded silk, without passing right through the fabric, and bring the needle out at an angle, a little further on, in the lining. Pass it back through the padded silk a little further on and bring the needle out at an angle by passing through the lining. Make the knot under the lining so that it is hidden.

→ *To make this work easier, you can buy a hat frame for a wide-brimmed hat from Artnuptia, or a similar specialist millinery supplier (like the tambourine for the bibi, page 66) and cover it with fabric. The work will be easier and quicker. Using the pre-fabricated hat frame, you can cut the brim to whatever width you like.*

→ *Depending on the fabric that you choose to make the wide-brimmed hat, the style of the hat will change radically. The same model of hat made in printed woollen fabric will make a nice winter hat, while black vinyl will give you a magnificent rain hat.*

2

THE BASIC TECHNIQUES

CUSTOMISATION

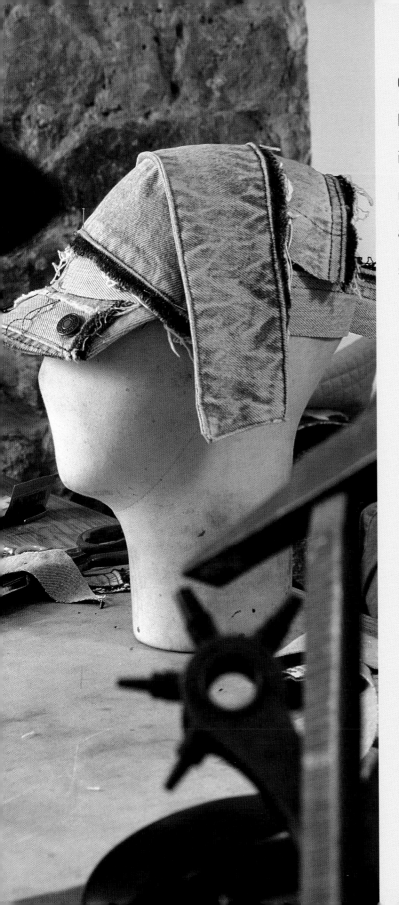

Giving new life to an item of clothing that you like, but of which you are slightly tired, is what fashion is all about. Customisation is a game of metamorphosis and personalisation that Estelle adores. She started young, by cutting into the sleeves of a kimono belonging to her mother (who was not all that keen on it) to create a garment to send to a fashion show... Using her own clothes and not those of her mother, Estelle now does this to her heart's content. On one of her skirts, she sewed some fabric samples taken from a supplier's testers. She has also transformed her Canadian shirt, from a lumberjack style to a chic jacket. Naturally, her feel for customisation is especially well-used in the art of millinery. She makes new hats from old fabric, worn-out denim or vintage lace. She also likes to renovate hats found in second-hand clothes shops or flea markets.

Woolly hat

What could be more ordinary than this woolly hat? You probably have a similar one in the back of your wardrobe. Yet, you could make something with it that is totally unique, by using beads or even artificial jewels...

1. You can liven up the knitted cabling with jade beads. Experiment with the positioning of the beads using long pins called T-pins.

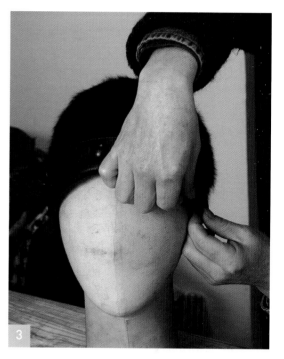

2. It is possible to change the style of a simple woolly hat – by moving the point towards the front and to one side, for example, to obtain a type of beret. To finish, Estelle decided to attach some large sequins, rather than beads. Cover the brim of the hat using 1m (39in) of sequins sewn to a strip of elastic bought from a haberdasher's.
Fold one end of the strip underneath to finish off the ribbon nicely. Sew this fold. Tack the ribbon to the hat, then sew it by taking in a stitch from the hat and a link of the sequinned elastic with each stitch.

3. You can also radically change a little angora hat by adding a leather trim. To attach leather to this type of hat, the knit will need to be a tight one. Sew the leather by machine, then add some grosgrain and fold the leather over it.

Remodelling a fedora

You often find fedoras in outlet stores or second-hand shops. The shape was created by the Italian Giuseppe Borsalino, who founded a large hat factory near Milan in the mid-nineteenth century. They are made from felt or even wool, like this fedora in merino wool, bought from a flea market, that Estelle has transformed by adding coloured pieces of leather.

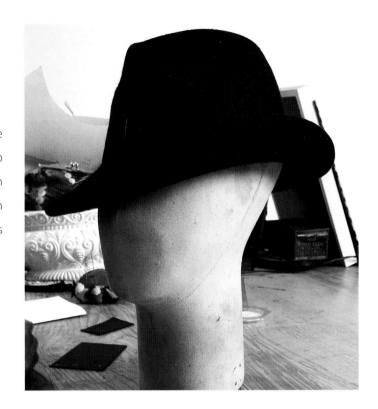

1. Cut out four patterns from pattern card: two patterns for cutting out the leather (a disc 7.5cm/3in in diameter and another 4.5cm/1¾in in diameter) and two smaller patterns for cutting shapes out of the fedora (a disc 6.5cm/2½in in diameter and another 3.5cm/1¼in in diameter). The difference in size will enable you to stick the leather discs inside the hat, putting the adhesive around the edge hidden by the merino wool.

→ *You can use star-shaped holes on this hat or flower shapes or even letters, as you wish. Cut out the patterns in the shape you want. The style of the hat will also vary depending on the material you use to fill the holes; you can choose to make the hat more feminine, more sophisticated or more sporty...*

1. Place the fedora on the dolly and try out the positions for the pieces you intend to cut out from the hat. Once you have made a decision, pin the patterns on to the hat and transfer the outline on to the hat using a pen.

→ *Leave a space between the various cut-outs, so that you have a wide enough margin on to which you can stick the piece of leather on the inside. If the cut-outs are too close together, the pieces of leather will overlap inside the hat and add thickness.*

Using a pair of fine-pointed scissors, cut out the merino wool by following the circles that you have drawn. To start cutting, put the point of the scissors into the surface of the hat inside the circle and then cut. Proceed slowly to avoid making a mistake.

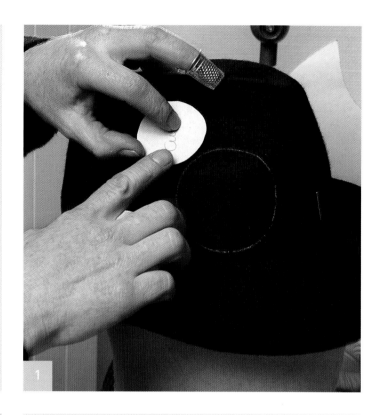

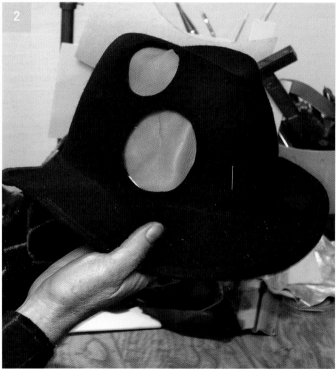

2. Before cutting the leather, try it out by slipping it inside the cut-out hat. Once you have chosen the colour for the discs, attach adhesive webbing to the leather to stiffen it. Transfer the patterns to the reverse of the leather with an ink pen in white, silver or gold, then cut out the pieces.

3. Before attaching the leather pieces, protect your work table with paper. Place the patterns for the shapes cut out from the hat on the right side of the leather pieces. Apply neoprene glue with a brush to the 5mm (¼in) border around the edge; this will be hidden inside the hat. Leave to dry.

Turn the hat inside out and place it on the sleeve board. Using a pen, draw a circle 5mm (¼in) outside the cut-out part. Apply a line of glue, making sure that you do not put glue over the edge of the cut-out circle, otherwise traces of glue will be visible from the outside. The neoprene glue requires both surfaces to be glued. Leave to dry.

When the neoprene glue is ready (this will be when it no longer sticks to your finger), place the disk inside the hat. It will stick immediately.

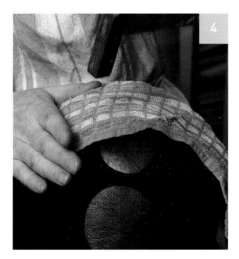

4. Place the hat on a hat block. Protect the pieces with a cloth and hammer to make sure that the glue sticks well.

→ *If excess glue appears on the outside of the hat, remove it with the point of a pin.*

5. To perfect the customisation of the hat, remove the sewing thread around the brim with a stitch-unpicker, then re-sew the brim with a thread that matches the shade of one of the pieces of leather. Here, Estelle has chosen a wine-coloured thread. Sew by placing the presser foot at the edge of the hat. Start at the centre back with a finishing-off stitch. Sew slowly, turning the hat as you go, and finish at the same place with another finishing-off stitch.

Cap made from a denim shirt

Using an old pair of jeans that no longer fits or a shirt that you no longer wear, you can make a cap based on the Lamineur model, designed by Estelle, which is similar to a miner's hat. By playing not only with the shape but also with the different shades of colour in the worn denim (light in parts exposed to the light and dark inside the pockets or at the seams), you can create a cap unlike any that has been seen before from this universal fabric made out of fustian from Nîmes. It is a durable cotton from which, originally, working clothes were made.

1 and 2. Using a stitch-unpicker, unpick the seams to give pieces of denim in various shades. Place the pieces of denim on the dolly and mark the various points (centre back, centre front, etc.).

Take the pattern for the visor of the Chinese-style cap to make the visor of the Lamineur. Cut two pieces of denim (the seam allowances are included in the pattern) and attach adhesive webbing to them.

→ *If possible, place the buttons on one of these pieces, or cut out another area with one or more buttons that you can sew on to one of the parts of the visor. Place the buttons parallel to the edge of the visor, but not too close to the edge, otherwise you will not be able to sew both parts of the visor when making it up.*

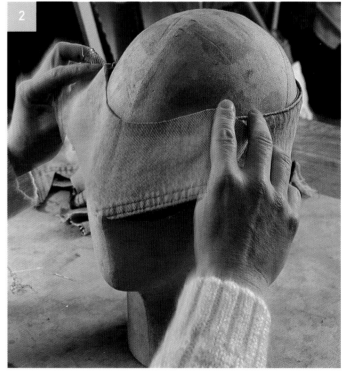

3 and 4. When joining together the piece decorated with buttons and the upper part of the visor, we recommend that you use a sewing machine intended for sewing leather, which enables you to use saddle stitch (a large stitch similar to the stitch used for denim seams). If you do not have access to such a machine, sew with a normal machine using cabled thread and a needle corresponding to the diameter of the thread (a normal thread might break when sewing denim).

Pin the two sides of the visor right sides together and join them by machine. Turn the visor right side out and iron using steam to flatten out the seams.

Using chalk, mark the headline on the visor 1.5cm (½in) from the edge. Sew by catching in both parts of the visor, then make notches around the headline. Pin the visor on the dolly.

1. Cut out a headband from the remaining shirt or jeans fabric. Here, Estelle has used three pieces to make the headband.

Using different pieces, experiment with making the crown of the cap by trying out various positions, colours and button location.

You can put a piece running from the forehead to the back of the head (here, the collar of a shirt), or line up the pieces on the visor, or even create some gaps, as shown here. Try on the cap in front of a mirror. If you are happy with the lay-out, you are ready to sew it.

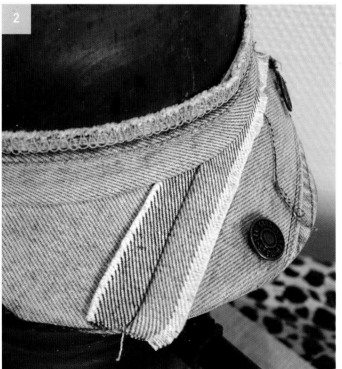

2. Join the three pieces for the headband by machine. Sew a joining seam at the ends, with a parallel line of stitching on either side. Iron open the seam allowances.

Pin the headband to the headline of the visor, matching up the edges (seam allowance included). Sew the headband to the visor by following the line of stitching already made on the visor around the headline. The difficult part here is sewing through all the layers of fabric without forming any folds, and you will need to sew slowly. Iron on the dolly.

3 and 4. Pin together the pieces that form the open crown of the cap. Start by joining the transverse band, made of three pieces of denim, using the machine.

Sew the front piece, with a button, to the transverse band. The line of sewing should follow the sewing that already exists on the transverse band. Do not sew over the headline; you will do this later by catching in the grosgrain at the headline.

Sew the back piece that links the transverse band to the centre back of the headband.

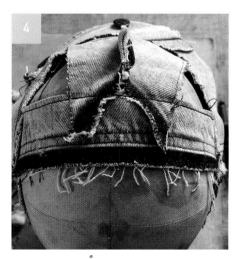

5. Attach a no. 5 grosgrain ribbon to the reverse of the headband. Pin the grosgrain at the headline, starting at the centre back. Tack and then sew by machine.

Place two no. 5 grosgrain ribbons side-by-side over the transverse band, holding them in place with a pin and then joining them together by sewing along the edge.

Open the double grosgrain and flatten the reverse side of the sewing using a small pair of scissors. Turn the grosgrain over and sew a row of stitching either side of the joining seam.

→ *If your denim band is as wide as a no. 9 grosgrain (4cm/1½in), attach a single piece of grosgrain in this size.*

Iron the grosgrain on the wrong side and pin it to the inside of the transverse denim band. Tack and sew the grosgrain on both sides to attach it firmly to the band.

Turn the grosgrain on the headband over the grosgrain on the transverse band and sew by machine.

Finish off the cap by snipping off any threads of denim (of course, you can leave a fringe of denim thread if you like).

3

THE BASIC TECHNIQUES

MAKING HAT FRAMES

This is how to make a chignon cap and a cloche using special millinery techniques that do not require either sewing or a pattern, but use a cast instead. The elasticity of the felt due to the density of the hair enables you to stretch it over a sparterie or a hat block with the aid of steam. The most common felt is made from rabbit hair, but there are also other types, determined by the nature of the hair used or its length. Moleskin, for example, has a velvety look and is one of the finest. It is made up of hair from the mole, otter, coypu or beaver.

With the velvet and snakeskin cloche, Estelle shows how to make a cast on the dolly. This time, the milliner is no longer working from a sparterie or a hat block, but she sculpts the hat directly on the model; this is a method that requires a lot of practice. Do not be disappointed if you do not succeed in making these two models at your first attempt.

Chignon cap in felt

The chignon cap is an accessory that, as its name indicates, is placed over a chignon, and can be worn on the side of the head or centred like that of a dancer. The chignon cap can also be worn like a bibi. Less obvious than a hat, the chignon cap enables you to hide a hairstyle, particularly if the hair is well pulled back, as with ballerinas.

1. Estelle has made a frame using gummed cloth. She has made it in jute that she has coated with a sparterie stiffener to make it solid, so that it can be used several times. The jute can be pinned easily, but you can also improvise a mould by using a bowl that will serve to cast a round chignon cap frame.
Cover the frame in a sheet of cling film. Obtain a manchon or a cone of felt. The manchon is easier to work with, but more difficult to find and a lot more expensive than the cone. Have to hand a basin of water and some T-pins.

2. Iron the felt by placing a wet cloth between the iron and the fabric, which will dampen the felt and make it more supple for stretching.

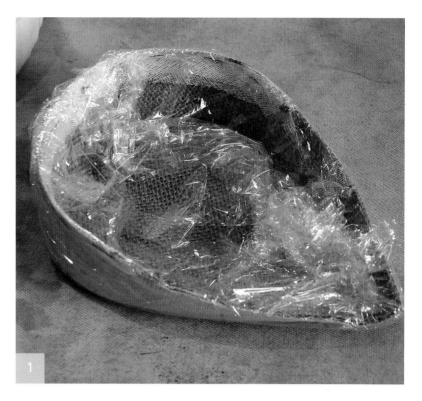

3. Loosen the felt by pulling it. The more steam that passes through the felt, the more it can be loosened and pulled out easily. Put the frame in the felt cone and continue to iron the felt around the frame using a cloth soaked in water.

4. Cut the felt around the frame leaving a 2cm (¾in) margin, which will be folded inside the chignon cap. Iron again with the damp cloth.

1. Turn up and pin the felt inside the frame using two T-pins. Insert the T-pins from the inside towards the outside. Do not place them on, or too close to, the rim of the chignon cap, otherwise they will not hold the felt firmly enough. Iron again, still using the wet cloth.

2. To prevent burning yourself while ironing, place a ball of paper or a pressing cushion against the edge of the chignon cap.

3. Place additional T-pins and continue to iron.
Spread the felt out over the fold with the aid of the steam. Remove the T-pins while stretching the felt. Eliminate any folds at the headline.
Also remove any excess felt with scissors, but leave at least 2cm (¾in) at the headline without any folds; this is where you will place a grosgrain ribbon.

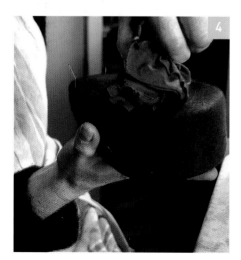

Brushing up gives the final finish to the stretching. To brush up the felt, place a wet cloth, rolled in a ball, on the soleplate of the iron. When it is full of steam, brush up the felt by turning the damp cloth anti-clockwise. Brush up all the parts that are visible.

→ *Instead of using a simple damp cloth, brush up the felt with a pressing cushion that you have made by forming a ball or a little cushion from scraps of fabric.*
Leave the felt to dry overnight, if possible near a radiator to speed up the drying process. The next day, remove the frame. Using a pair of scissors, cut leaving a 2cm (¾in) turn-up inside the chignon cap. At the point, leave just 1cm (½in) of turn-up, otherwise it will be very thick. Fold and slit the turn-up in the middle to obtain a very sharp point.

5. Using a paintbrush, daub the inside of the chignon cap with an alcohol-based sizing. This is for making felt, straw and fabric rigid (in the past, gum arabic was used).

Apply the sizing sparingly to the flat surface and at the edges, where the shape must remain very rigid.

Put the chignon cap back on the frame, attach it with some pins and leave to dry. Sew three pieces of hat elastic at the top and to the sides of the chignon cap (see how to attach elastic to the bibi, page 73), then cover them with a grosgrain ribbon around the head opening (even if the chignon cap is simply placed on the head, it should still have grosgrain ribbon attached to the inside). The loops of elastic that overhang the grosgrain will be used to hold the chignon cap in place with hair pins.

6. Decorate the chignon cap with a motif cut from tartan. Stiffen the fabric first with adhesive webbing. Using pattern card, make a template of the motif (flower, letter, etc.). Here, Estelle has chosen a spade. Cut out and then pin the fabric motif to the chignon cap before sewing with invisible stitches (though they can be visible inside the chignon cap). Decorate the edge of the spade with matching glitter, in a similar manner to the crown of flowers (see pages 42–43).

Cloche

The cloche, worn by music-hall dancers in the 1920s, evokes the boyish hairstyles of the time and is one of Estelle's favourite hats; it is made here using silk velvet and lacquered python skin.

MAKING THE FRAME

1. The shell of the cloche is made from gummed cloth, i.e. stiffened jute. The shell comprises a crown and a band. To make it, you will need approximately 1m (39in) of gummed cloth (you should be able to cover all of your dolly). Here, the cloche is made for a head circumference of 57cm (22½in).

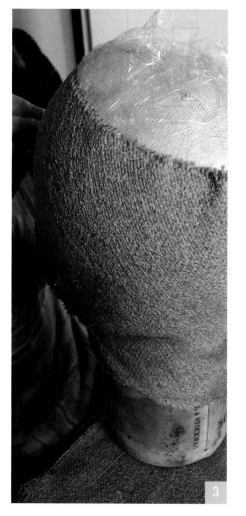

2 and 3. Cut two strips of cloth, 25cm (9¾in) in depth, on the bias for the band and the crown. Iron the first strip with a wet cloth to make it very moist.

Protect the dolly with cling film, then cover it with the strip of cloth. Cover the nape of the neck with cloth too, as, when worn, the cloche will hug the curve of the neck.

Attach the cloth to the dolly with T-pins.

Iron using steam, stretching the cloth so that it hugs the shape of the dolly. The more you stretch the cloth using steam, the more the bias web of the cloth will tighten, which will prevent it from going out of shape later.

4 and 5. Stitch together the band using linen thread and a milliner's needle. Sew directly on the dolly using cross stitch; for each stitch, catch in the two thicknesses of gummed cloth, but be careful not to include either the dolly or the cling film.

6. Glaze the seams with a very hot iron (thermostat set to maximum); glazing fabric is done by ironing it and making it shiny. Here, ironing will also flatten out the seams. Do this by moving the iron in a circular motion over the seams until you can no longer feel the raised sewing beneath your fingers.

Take the second strip and iron it with a wet cloth to make it very moist. Cover the skull of the dolly with a piece of cloth for the crown and attach the cloth using T-pins.

1. Cut off the excess, leaving 2cm (¾in) of cloth overhanging the band all round.

Iron with a very hot iron. Smooth out the excess fabric around the edge of the crown by stretching it, and then join the crown to the band with cross stitches.

→ *The cloth dries very quickly (it is therefore difficult to get a needle through it); soften it as often as necessary using the iron so that you can sew it more easily.*

Use a very hot iron to glaze the seams once more using a circular motion, as before.

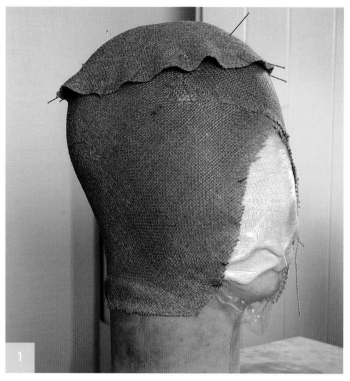

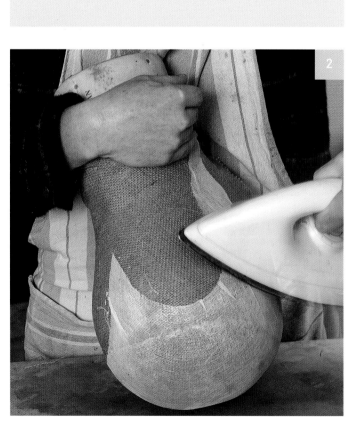

2. Take 1m (39in) of *singalette* (a stiffened muslin sold by the metre) on a roll 70cm (27½in) in width. The muslin is used here to even out the jute that you have been working with. For the crown, cut out a triangle with 30cm (12in) sides on the bias of the muslin. Dampen the triangle with a wet cloth, place it on the crown and iron very quickly with a very hot iron (thermostat set to maximum), so that it hugs the head of the dolly well. You need to iron very quickly, as the muslin, being a stiffened fabric, will stick to the iron easily. Iron and stretch the muslin so that the web of the fabric tightens correctly. Iron the points of the triangle well.

→ *The muslin dries very quickly, so moisten it as you go with a little water.*

→ *Use the lightest iron possible, as the work is hard and very physical. Also, do not use the iron that you usually use for delicate fabrics, as this work on the cloche wears out the soleplate.*

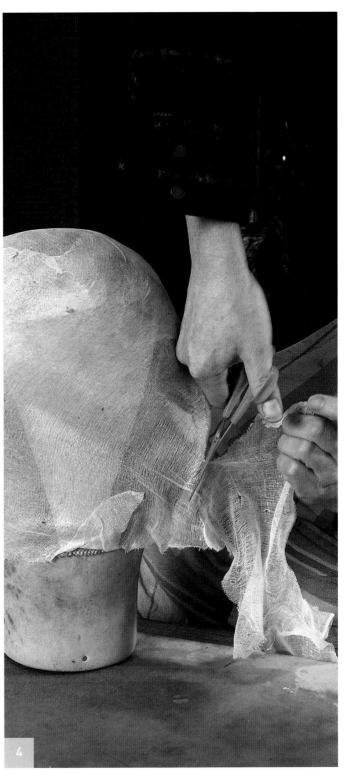

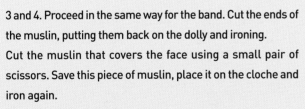

3 and 4. Proceed in the same way for the band. Cut the ends of the muslin, putting them back on the dolly and ironing.

Cut the muslin that covers the face using a small pair of scissors. Save this piece of muslin, place it on the cloche and iron again.

Leave to dry overnight.

TURNING OUT

1. Using a pair of scissors, cut the cloche at the face in a line running from the forehead to the chin.

Slide a piece of old corset boning between the cloche and the model until you feel the cloche coming away from the dolly. Mark the centre back and centre front points with a pencil, then remove.

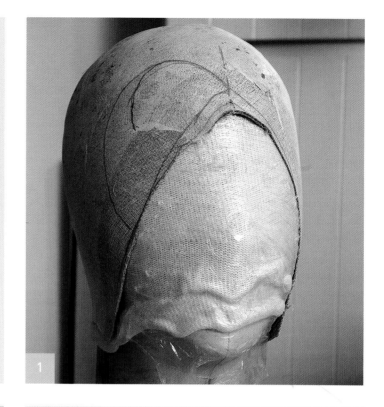

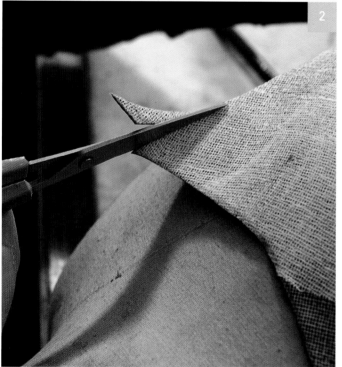

2. Replace the cloche on the dolly. Using a pencil, draw the outline around the face and over the nape of the neck. At this stage, you must decide on the style of the cloche. For example, you could make a fringe or cut out the shape of a heart, as shown here.

Cut out the shape using a small pair of scissors.

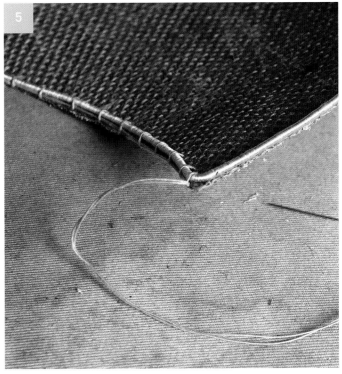

3, 4 and 5. Attach a millinery wire all around the edge of the cloche. Use a solid (no. 7) millinery wire, some linen thread and a fur needle or a no. 7 milliner's needle.

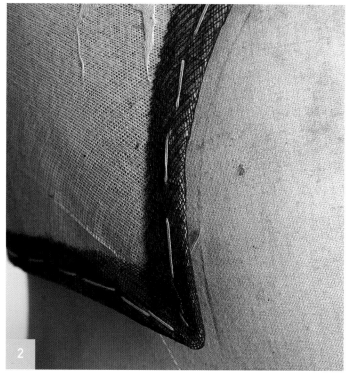

1. Cut out a 10cm (4in) wide strip of *singalette* (muslin) on the bias and pull until the width is no more than 5cm (2in). Place it around the rim of the cloche and pin at the centre back and centre front.

2. Sew the muslin with linen thread and a fur needle. Sew a normal running stitch, passing through the cloche with each stitch.
Iron the sewing.

3 and 4. Make a crown and a band in black flannelette. Attach the crown with linen thread, then sew the band, turning it under the edges of the cloche.

5. Pin the first piece of black, lacquered python skin across the cloche. Using a fur needle and linen thread, sew the python skin to the cloche (passing through the cloche with each stitch).

Take 50cm (19¾in) of black silk velvet on a 120cm (47¼in) roll, cut on the full bias. Try out positions on the dolly to determine the size of the piece that you will need to cover one side of the cloche. Cut the velvet and pin it along the python skin, folding the edge underneath. Smooth out the fullness to avoid folds.

Sew the velvet using slip stitch and a no. 7 milliner's needle and black cotton thread, passing through the cloche with each stitch. Start from the inside and return using a tiny stitch on the fold of the velvet.

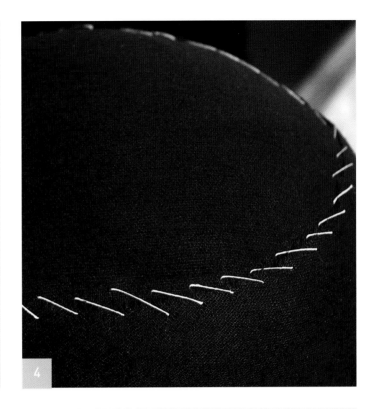

In the same way, place a second piece of black python skin and a second piece of velvet on the other side of the cloche. When finished, the cloche will be completely covered with these two materials.

For the lining inside the cloche, use satin acetate. Cut a lining made up of a crown and a band in the same measurements as the cloche. Pin, adjusting the measurements of the lining as you go. Join the crown and the band of the lining using the sewing machine.

Attach the lining to the inside of the cloche by sewing by hand. Follow the rim of the cloche exactly, ensuring that you do not go over it.

THE CREATIVE ARTIST

THE HATS CREATED IN THE WORKSHOP AND ON DISPLAY IN THE WINDOW CAN BE BOUGHT WITH A MATCHING SCARF, CHOKER OR BAG, EITHER ON THE SPUR OF THE MOMENT OR AS A CONSIDERED PURCHASE. THE HATS LEAVE ON THE HEADS OF THEIR NEW OWNERS, OR THEY ARE CARRIED AWAY IN A BAG – THE HAT STUFFED WITH TISSUE PAPER TO PREVENT IT FROM LOSING ITS SHAPE IN TRANSIT.

<Crown of flowers

This floral headpiece, with flowers cut from the same material as the fabric that makes the headband, is a complete reworking of the concept of the crown. This original creation shows the wealth of possibilities available using any fabrics printed with a floral motif, such as summer-weight cotton fabric, as shown here, or silks, or satins, etc.

TECHNIQUES USED
• cut and sewn, pages 32–43

>Chinese-style cap

By combining an elegant fabric (a toile de Jouy is used here) with the shape of a military cap, Estelle shows how to play with the juxtaposition of shapes and materials. This design can be made with other elegant fabrics: tartan or hound's-tooth, silks, lamés, etc.

TECHNIQUES USED
• cut and sewn, pages 44–59

<Beret

Structured by adding a headband, this beret has an unexpected finish. By tilting it over the forehead, tipping it backwards or to one side, the same beret can take on many different styles.

TECHNIQUES USED

• cut and sewn, pages 60–65

>Bibi

Using woollen fabric, instead of silk or satin, gives the bibi a modern, unexpected look that makes it easier to wear day-to-day. This model uses a hat frame bought in a shop.

TECHNIQUES USED

• cut and sewn, pages 66–73

<Wide-brimmed hat

The wide-brimmed hat, made from silk and decorated with a grosgrain ribbon, remains a millinery classic, particularly suitable for marriages and receptions. For everyday wear, make this wide-brimmed hat in modern materials, such as vinyl, tartan or denim.

TECHNIQUES USED
• cut and sewn, pages 74–85

>Woolly hat

You can make several styles of hat using the same woolly hat as a basis, e.g. something for an evening out or for a whole season. Estelle regularly updates her collection of woolly hats by adding sequins, flowers, shells, beads, jewels or even charms.

TECHNIQUES USED
• customisation, page 88

<Fedora

To give new life to an old hat, you should not hesitate to cut into it. By cutting bits out of a fedora, Estelle shows how you can brighten up an austere hat.

TECHNIQUES USED
• customisation, pages 89–91

>Cloche

The cloche, a favourite of the music halls in the period between the wars, is one of the most difficult types of hat to make. The milliner's art culminates in making this shell, moulded on a model and covered with silk velvet and lacquered python skin.

TECHNIQUES USED
• making hat frames, pages 102–109

MILLINERY TERMS

Band: curved part of a pattern usually used for making the sides of a hat.

Barder: reinforcing a hat block by covering it with pieces of the same material. A sparterie can be made more solid with pieces of gummed cloth to make it almost as resilient as a hat block.

Bias: the crosswise direction of a fabric in relation to the straight grain. Webbing and fabrics are always used on the bias in millinery, as the elasticity of material cut on the bias enables it to mould to the shape of the head.

Blockmaker: someone who makes blocks for making hats and shoes.

Brim: the edge of a hat.

Cabled thread: very thick thread made up of several threads joined together.

Camion: a little needle used to hold rolls of grosgrain ribbon in place.

Cannetille: fine millinery wire. Depending on its thickness, the wire is called *bord* (the thickest of the wires), *barrette* (average width wire), *coulisse* (fine), *cannetill* or *cannelette* (very fine wire in gold or silver colour).

Centre back: the point on a hat corresponding to the back of the head, diametrically opposite the centre front.

Centre front: the point on a hat coinciding with the centre of the head at the front.

Centre side: a point situated approximately above the ears, in the centre of the headband or band going from the centre front to the centre back.

Chalk hem marker: chalk combined with a reservoir used for marking fabric. It is filled with talc, which can be rubbed away easily without leaving any trace on the fabric.

Chien: a double brush used when working with felt.

Cone: piece of felt in a conical shape.

Coq: iron made up of a stem and an egg-shaped end.

Coquage: manipulation that consists of stretching hot material using a *coq*.

Crin: tube or synthetic ribbon for structuring hats and decorating them. Crins are often used for wedding hats.

Crown: the part of the hat that encases the head. It is made up of sides (vertical) and a crown tip (horizontal). It is also the shape of a hat when reduced to a single crown.

Crown tip: the flat top of the hat.

Curling: process of making grosgrain ribbon curl using steam, known as curling the grosgrain.

Finishing-off stitch: sewing back and forth on the sewing machine to finish off the thread, i.e. to prevent the sewing from unravelling. In general, a line of sewing or topstitching always begins and ends with a finishing-off stitch.

Grosgrain: grosgrain is a wide ribbon, used both as a base material in millinery and as a decorative element.

Gummed cloth: stiffened jute.

Hat block or wood block: hat block, generally made from lime tree wood, used for making hats.

Hat stretcher: tool made from wood and metal for enlarging a hat.

Head opening or headline: the part of the hat where the head enters. The head opening is defined and protected by the grosgrain around it.

Millinery wire: malleable combination of copper and zinc. It comes in various diameters (see *cannetille*).

Notching: cutting out triangular shapes from fabric edges using two snips of the scissors. The notches serve as marking points.

Pattern: model or template in card or paper.

Presser foot: part of the sewing machine that passes over the fabric. The presser foot is made up of two parallel branches between which the needle sews.

Pressing cushion: ball of wool or a small cushion placed under the fabric when ironing or brushing up felt.

Selvage: the finished edge of a fabric.

Singalette: a type of starched muslin.

Sparterie: wooden framework covered with a stiffened muslin weave that milliners make themselves when creating a hat. Originally, the hat block was covered with overlapping pieces of sparterie. As sparteries are difficult to find today, you can make a hat block using gummed cloth reinforced with millinery wire and adhesive.

Stiffener: substance for strengthening straw, felt and fabric. Stiffeners can be made from gum arabic, gelatine, or have an alcohol base. They are applied with a paintbrush or a sponge. In the past, a milliner specialising in stiffeners would focus solely on this task.

Stitch-unpicker: a tool with a forked end, for undoing stitching. The longest prong is bevelled and sharp.

Straw: plaited vegetable or synthetic fibres. Straw is sold in ribbons or as straw laize, which come in wide widths like fabrics.

T-pin: long, flexible pin that it is possible to bend.

Tacking: temporary sewing with large stitches, using normal thread or tacking thread.

TABLE OF CONTENTS

ACKNOWLEDGEMENTS AND CREDITS

The authors dedicate this book to their mothers.

Fabienne Gambrelle dedicates this work to the memory of Nicole Gambrelle,
who was a milliner in her own way, for she was just as good at dressmaking as she was at embroidery and knitting.

Estelle Ramousse dedicates this work to Danielle Ramousse, and to Yvonne Guérin, her great-aunt, to Christiane and
Marinette Bernardini, who taught her the trade and to Virginie de Broc, who took over from them.

Fabienne Gambrelle and Estelle Ramousse would like to thank artist/painter Philippe Barnier, who facilitated their
meeting and who allowed some filming to be done at his home, for which he lent his canvases (www.barnier.com).

As well as the photographer, Florent de La Tullaye, they would also like to thank Madame Galanter, who kindly
welcomed them into her workshop, as well as the team at Artnuptia, where the photos were taken, and the models
Amélie Airiau, Marie D., Corinne Ducos and Sixtine Deroure.

On pages 8, 11 and 13, Bridgeman-Giraudon documents; pages 14–15, Lapi/Roger-Viollet document.

First published in Great Britain 2010 by Search Press Limited,
Wellwood, North Farm Road, Tunbridge Wells, Kent TN2 3DR

Published originally under the title: 'Secrets d'ateliers – Les chapeaux'

Copyright © 2007 by Editions Solar, Paris

English translation copyright © 2010 Search Press Limited

English translation by Cicero Translations

English edition edited and typeset by GreenGate Publishing Services

All rights reserved. No part of this book, text, photographs or illustrations may be reproduced or transmitted in any
form or by any means by print, photoprint, microfilm, microfiche, photocopier, internet or in any way known or as yet
unknown, or stored in a retrieval system, without written permission obtained beforehand from Search Press.

ISBN: 978-1-84448-505-5

Graphic design and production (French edition): Guylaine Moi
Photoengraving: Point 4

Printed in Malaysia